NOTTINGHAMSHIRE WALKS

Jubilee Guide Book

The walks in this publication have been compiled by members of the Ramblers'
Association – Nottinghamshire Area as their contribution to the Ramblers'
Diamond Jubilee Celebrations

Editor: Chris Thompson (Area Footpaths Secretary)

Maps: Jeff Nightingale

Published by
CORDEE – LEICESTER

Copyright Ramblers' Association, Nottinghamshire Area 1995

ISBN: 1 871890 77 2

Reprinted 2001

British Library Cataloguing Publication Data

A catalogue record for this book is available from the British Library

We hope this Guide will enable and encourage people to enjoy walking some of the footpaths in Nottinghamshire, and thus help to preserve these paths for future generations.
Although every effort has been made to keep the Guide as clear and accurate as possible, we are sorry that we cannot take any responsibility for your walks or wanderings, so please take care.

All trade enquiries to Cordee, 3a de Montfort Street, Leicester LE1 7HD

This book is available from specialist equipment shops and booksellers in the area. It can, along with all the maps mentioned in the text, be obtained from the publishers. Please write for a copy of our comprehensive stocklist of outdoor recreation and travel books and maps, or visit our website www.cordee.co.uk

Cover photographs by Gordon Gadsby Beeston

Printed and bound in Great Britain by

The Guernsey Press Co. Ltd, Guernsey, Channel Islands

CONTENTS

NEW ORDNANCE SURVEY MAPS

The OS. Pathfinder Maps listed for each of the 60 Walks in this book, are no longer published. The Ordnance Survey have replaced them with the new Explorer Series at a scale of 1:25 000 (orange covers). The maps now recommended for the 60 Walks in this book are:

Explorer Map 269 – Chesterfield & Alfreton
Walks: 23. 24. 25.

Explorer Map 270 (28) – Sherwood Forest
Walks: 13. 14. 15. 16. 22. 26. 27. 28. 29. 30. 38. 42. 43.

Explorer Map 271 – Newark on Trent
Walks: 5. 6. 7. 9. 10. 11. 12. 17. 18. 19. 20. 21. 31. 32. 33. 34. 35. 36. 37.

Explorer Map 260 – Nottingham
Walks: 38. 39. 40. 41. 42. 43. 44. 45. 46. 47. 48. 49. 50. 51. 52. 53. 54. 55. 56. 57.

Explorer Map 246 – Loughborough
Walks: 56. 58. 59. 60.

Explorer Map 279 – Doncaster
Walks: 3. 4. 8.

Explorer Map 280 – Isle of Axholme
Walks: 1. 2.

FOREWORD

This book celebrates 60 years of work by the Ramblers' Association for walkers. Throughout the book, the concerns of the Ramblers can clearly be seen - encouraging people to enjoy the countryside; the need for clear, unobstructed paths; and the right to roam through open uncultivated countryside.

The Nottinghamshire landscape tends to be undervalued. Over recent years, I've increasingly walked the footpath network in the county. The walks in this book have extended my range. They take in all corners of Nottinghamshire; town and country; go through forest into heathland; visit the Trent and other Nottinghamshire rivers. I've enjoyed many of these walks and so has my family.

I hope you'll not only share my enjoyment, but also take steps to protect and enhance our countryside. Last year, the Ramblers' Association played an important part in stopping the privatisation of the Forestry Commission, thus preserving the right to roam through our woodland. Another achievement would be to ensure that the millions of pounds that landowners receive in grant from government at both Westminster and Brussels actually raised the landscape and environment whilst giving public access to enjoy it.

I wish the Ramblers' Association many more years of enjoyable walking and successful campaigning.

Paddy Tipping MP
President Nottinghamshire Area Ramblers
24th March, 1995

PREFACE

What better way could there be to celebrate the 60 years since the founding of the Ramblers' Association (R.A.) in 1935 than to offer 60 good walks within the county? And how better to do this than to invite its local groups to design and describe favourite walks from their own locality?

This book is the result. Most of the walks are of the right length for a morning or afternoon; they are spread across the county, as you can see from the index map on page xx and they highlight its variety, from the Trent plain or rolling farmland to heritage trails in four Nottinghamshire towns.

We are sorry but we can't say that all these walks will suit everyone. Being on the eastern side of the Pennines, we have a reasonably dry climate, ideal for arable crops. So, many paths cross or skirt ploughed fields. Walking can be difficult, especially if the farmer has failed to "re-instate" the path, as he is supposed to do under the 1990 Rights of Way Act.

Ramblers appreciate the countryside tended by farmers and landowners. Good husbandry is what gives the English landscape its particular beauty, so we are grateful for their stewardship. The network of paths and bridleways is part of everyone's heritage, bequeathed to us all by town and country dwellers from past centuries. Unfortunately, not all farmers play their part in protecting this heritage, so the R.A. campaigns to ensure that this precious network can be enjoyed by everyone. We welcome the Countryside Commission's target of making all rights of way usable by the new millenium and collaborate to achieve it.

Nottinghamshire R.A. members also appreciate the work of the county Highway Authority in maintaining bridges and stiles; of their Rights of Way section in dealing with matters when legal or planning problems arise and in the work of Leisure Services in publicising the attractions of the Nottinghamshire countryside, through walks and cycle leaflets and through the Guided Walks programme, in collaboration with the R.A.

This book could not have been produced without the work of many of our members. Warmest thanks are due to: local groups who responded so enthusiastically to this Jubilee project; to the many individuals who volunteered to test the walks on the ground (mostly during a particularly wet winter!); to our President, for the Foreword and his support for the Association in the county and in

vii

Westminster; to Sue and Phil Andrews who typed up the descriptions; to Jeff Nightingale who contributed the maps and artwork; to Area Committee Member Reg Simpson; to Mansfield District Council for the Mansfield Heritage Walk and Bassetlaw District Council for the Worksop and Retford Heritage Walks; to Marian Staniforth of Nottingham Group and Joan Mankelow, Keith Johnson and Trevor Bagshaw of Broxtowe Group for checking the routes; to Area Officers Malcolm Mackenzie, Geoff Rix and Alex Staniforth, who have had a substantial editorial involvement and above all to Chris Thompson, who took on this project on top of his very busy role as our Footpaths Officer. Most people probably do not realise how much work is covered by Chris and members of the Footpaths Sub-Committee.

We are delighted to offer these walks for your enjoyment. You will need to keep your wits about you because the English style of waymarking is to provide the minimum: we are not keen on having so many signs that the walker stops thinking! If you take one of the walks in this book you will be joining thousands of others in one of the most popular and relaxing pursuits. And if you join the R.A. (details on page xiii) you will be joining more than 2000 people in Nottinghamshire who have done so, to help make a walk in the countryside possible and enjoyable for themselves and succeeding generations. Walk in Nottinghamshire! You will find it irresistible!

Derrick Fielden

Nottinghamshire Area Chairman

EDITOR'S NOTES

Welcome to 60 Nottinghamshire Walks. We (the Ramblers' Association Nottinghamshire Area) have taken the opportunity to celebrate our Jubilee Year (1995) by writing this book of theme walks to promote our county.

In addition to the 60 theme walks we have also included six Heritage Walks around our principal Nottinghamshire towns and the City of Nottingham, as well as full tourist information and places to visit to complement your walks. Indeed, you could say you have here a walking encyclopaedia of Nottinghamshire walking!

As the Editor of this project it has been a great pleasure to work with so many enthusiastic R.A. members. Thanks are expressed by our Chairman to you all, but I must thank all the Nottinghamshire R.A. Groups and many individual members for all their assistance in the many tasks involved in compiling this book: describing the walks, testing the routes, walking, collating items of historical interest, typing, map drawing, etc. Indeed, without all your help this project would never have been completed. I would like to thank and name so many people, but I must name four people in particular: Sue and Phil Andrews for the typing and assistance in logging the points of interest section, Jeff Nightingale for the drawing of the maps and Malcolm Mackenzie for the inclusion of several of his walks. A big "thank you" to all the many people involved in the project.

However, before setting out on these walks, I wish to emphasize a few points. Firstly, we describe as accurately as possible 60 theme walks and 6 Heritage walks that, in our view, maintain a legal line of access (definitive path). Occasionally we use permissive paths (written on maps), which are not, in our view, legal lines but are regularly walked. In a few cases we have some local footpath problems. In these cases, we describe a permissive path in order to enable you to continue your walk. We shall in these cases continue to work closely with the Highways Authority to have the definitive line reinstated.

Each walk includes a hand-drawn map. We must emphasize these maps are **for guidance** *only*. We recommend that you purchase Ordnance Survey maps and before embarking on a walk, follow the route over with your map. All the walks have been based on a pace of 30 minutes per mile, which is a family walking speed. Please remember to follow the Country Code when out walking and should you experience problems on the walks by obstructions, cropping, ploughing, misleading notices, lack of way-marking, aggressive bulls in fields, difficulty by landowners or their agents, locked gates, broken bridges or stiles, please report these details to the Senior Footpath Officer, Planning & Economic Development, Nottinghamshire County Council, Trent Bridge House, West Bridgford, Nottingham NG2 6BJ (Tel. (0115) 971 4483) who will take the necessary action.

I now hope that you, the walker, will have many pleasurable hours of enjoyment exploring our county's countryside as a result of this hard work, and look forward to meeting many of you on the paths very soon.

Chris Thompson

Nottinghamshire Area R.A. Footpaths Secretary

A SHORT HISTORY OF THE RAMBLERS' ASSOCIATION

This year, 1995, the Ramblers' celebrate their 60th Anniversary. From its formation in 1935, it has achieved a great deal for Britain's walkers. The foundations for the Association can be traced back to the early part of the 19th century: indeed, the first known society dedicated to footpath preservation was established in 1824 in York. The ensuing years saw the formation of various like-minded bodies throughout Great Britain and by the 1920's and early 1930's many rambling clubs, footpath societies and preservation societies were in existence. It was also in this period that the campaign for public access became a prominent feature and was a key factor in the setting up of the Ramblers' Association. The famous (or infamous) mass trespass on Kinder Scout in 1932 was the culmination of this issue.

Before the present day Association came into being, there existed the precursor in the shape of the National Council of Ramblers' Federation. Having been formed in 1931, its existence was short-lived because in 1935 they changed their name to the Ramblers' Association. This was to be a national organisation and it began the immediate task of lobbying for access to the hills, as well as for long-distance paths, national parks and better protection for public rights of way.

Mention must be made of one personality who, above all others, stands out in the cause of promoting the great outdoors: Tom Stephenson. He had long advocated many of the ideals which were to become the cornerstones of the Ramblers'; and he will always be remembered as the instigator of that most famous of long-distance paths: the Pennine Way. He served the Ramblers' for many years as the first full-time Secretary.

Though the Second World War intervened, much was proposed to set the Association in the forefront of caring for the interests of walkers. Some of the major milestones include:

- In the 1940's, The Ramblers' spearheaded a campaign which led to the creation of national parks and long-distance paths and the recording of rights of way.

- In the 1960's, The Ramblers' persuaded the Ordnance Survey to show rights of way on OS maps.

- From the 1960's on, The Ramblers' detailed plans for the designation of long-distance paths such as the Pennine Way and the Cotswold Way turned into reality.

- From the 1970's, The Ramblers' were the first to criticise tax concessions for conifer afforestation, which damages wildlife and scenery. These concessions were abolished in 1988.

- In 1981, during the passage of the Wildlife and Countryside Act, The Ramblers' lobbying protected objectors' right of appeal against proposals to close rights of way.

- The Ramblers' played a leading role in securing the Rights of Way Act 1990, which at last provides legislation to deal effectively with illegal ploughing and cropping of footpaths.

- And recently The Ramblers' led national campaigns to persuade the government not to jeopardize freedom to roam on Forestry Commission land.

Much has happened since that decision was taken 60 years ago to form the Ramblers' Association: much remains to be done. So as the celebrations unfold to commemorate the 60th Anniversary, it is sobering to reflect on what state our countryside would be today if it were not for the campaigning and commitment of the Ramblers Association. Walkers have a lot to thank them for.

Alex Staniforth

Area Secretary: Nottinghamshire

RAMBLERS' ASSOCIATION CONTACTS

National Office

Ramblers' Association,
1-5 Wandsworth Road,
London SW8 2XX

Tel. no. (0171) 582-6878
Fax no. (0171) 587-3799

Local R.A. Contacts

Area Secretary: Mr. Alex Staniforth,
                               2 Park View,
                               Mapperley,
                               Nottingham NG3 5FD

Area Footpaths Secretary: Mr. Chris Thompson,
                               21 Spindle View,
                               Calverton,
                               Nottingham NG14 6HF

Local R.A. Groups

Group	Area
Broxtowe	Broxtowe District
Collingham	Collingham area
Dukeries	Ollerton/Edwinstowe area
Gedling	Gedling District (excluding Ravenshead)
Harworth & Bircotes	Harworth & Bircotes area
Mansfield	Group in the process of being formed
Newark	Newark area
Nottingham	City of Nottingham
Ravenshead	Ravenshead District
Retford	Retford area
Rushcliffe	District of Rushcliffe (excluding Bottesford area)
Southwell	Southwell area
Vale of Belvoir	Based on Bottesford area
Worksop	Worksop area

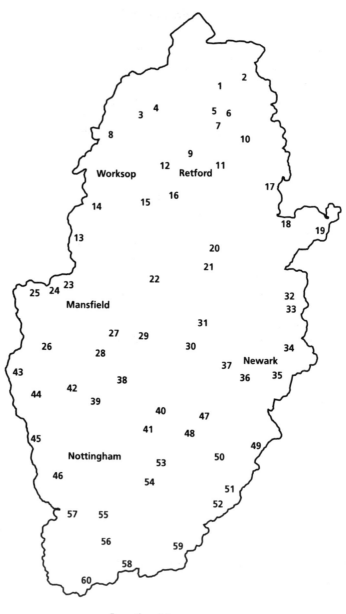

Location Map

THE WALKS

THE COUNTY OF NOTTINGHAMSHIRE

Situated in the heart of England, Nottinghamshire's charms are both subtle and understated, but nevertheless well-worth seeking out. The visitor enters a land full of reminders of our past, a land of pine forests, productive farmland and wooded parklands of the great estates.

The County's most famous son is, of course, Robin Hood, and there are reminders of his presence all over - from the Castle itself, the safe bastion of the Sheriff, to the Major Oak deep in the heart of Sherwood Forest, of which some 450 acres remain. The burial site of Will Scarlet, the chapel where Robin was said to have married Marian, remains of King John's Palace and links with Friar Tuck, all these may be found on walks through the County.

The City itself is a centre for history, culture, shopping and sport. Our industrial past can be traced at the Lace Hall, Ruddington Framework Knitters' Museum, Papplewick Pumping Station, Wollaton Industrial Museum and Green's Windmill. Giants of literature may be examined at Newstead, home of Lord Byron and Eastwood, the birthplace of D.H. Lawrence. Religious buildings abound, including Southwell Minster with its incomparable chapter house. Other religious movements whose founders originated in the county include the Pilgrim Fathers, the Methodists and Quakers.

The historic town of Newark, with its ruined castle, was besieged for four years by Cromwell's forces in the English Civil War. Nottingham itself boasts a complex system of caves, which may be visited, together with the prehistoric cave dwellings to be found at Creswell Crags. Country houses are open at Rufford, Newstead, Wollaton and there are many centres where old crafts are revived and preserved, such as at Longdale and Edwinstowe. Horticulturally, the County boasts some lovely gardens, such as at Hodsock Priory; and Southwell was the birthplace of the Bramley apple. Laxton offers a unique opportunity to see a Medieval open field system of farming still practised today.

Our footpaths and bridleways are generally well-maintained, with a careful watch kept on their preservation. They span a varied countryside taking in farmland, canals, rivers, fine villages and woodland. The walks in this book have been compiled by the Groups within the Nottinghamshire Area and reflect the wide variety of countryside, terrain, scenery and points of interest to be found around the county. Many of the features mentioned above can be visited when following the walks. Above all, you may be sure of a welcome worthy of the heart of the country.

Happy Rambling!

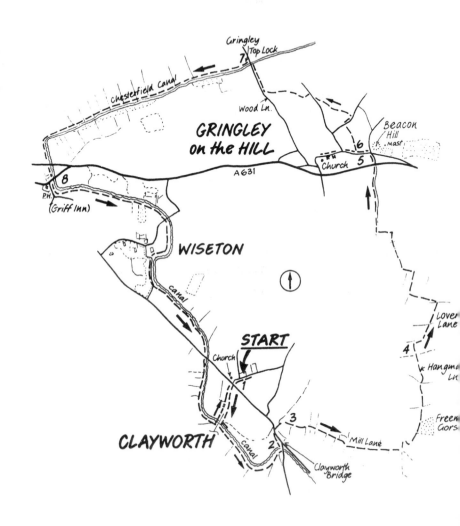

WALK 1

1. North Nottinghamshire Beacon and Cuckoo

A beautiful circular walk using one of the most attractive stretches of the Chesterfield Canal and linking the villages of Clayworth, Gringley on the Hill and Wiseton.

THE FACTS

Area: Clayworth, Gringley on the Hill, Wiseton

Distance: 11.5 km (7 miles)

Duration: 3.5 hours

Maps Required: OS Pathfinder 728 (SK 69/79) Harworth & Gringley on the Hill and 745 (SK 68/78) East Retford (North) & Blyth

                     OS Landranger 112 Scunthorpe & 120 Mansfield & Worksop

Bus/Train Link: Retford/Gainsborough

Terrain: Canal towpath, green lanes, some field paths

Starting Point: Grass verge, Church Lane, Clayworth SK 726884

Refreshments: Several public houses in Clayworth, Gringley on the Hill and the Griff Inn, Drakeholes

THE ROUTE

1.   After parking your car in Church Lane, return to St. Nicholas' Church in Town Street. At the junction cross the road along St. Peter's Lane going past Royston Manor, a Victorianised Tudor house, now a restaurant. On reaching the canal, go over the bridge and take the towpath to the left. Follow the canal until you reach the next bridge (Clayworth Bridge).

1

2.   Leave the canal and turn left back along Town Street towards Clayworth, but cross the road before the Brewer's Arms to take the road on the right (Mill Lane).

3.   You continue along Mill Lane turning right at the junction and passing Mill House. After 1.3 km you reach a junction of paths (note Trent Valley Way sign: a wavy blue arrow) where we turn left. We are now going along Hangman's Lane. Follow a clear path firstly along a green lane into a field, turning right to follow the field edge path to become a green lane again and continue along this to reach the top of the hill.

4.   You are now in a wide grassy area. Turn right and then left into a tree-covered lane (Lovers' Lane). Follow an obvious path to reach a ditchboard at the end of the enclosed area. Enter an open field, turn left and follow the field edge path around two fields to reach the tarmac road (Lancaster Road). Follow this to reach the A631, cross the road **with care** and walk into Gringley on the Hill. At the crossroads on the right there is a gate access onto Beacon Hill. After visiting Beacon Hill, return to the crossroads.

5.   Our walk continues along High Street to take the path through a kissing-gate on the right just after passing the Manor House. Refreshments are available at the Blue Bell Inn, reached by continuing along the High Street. This would also be an opportunity to visit the Church of St. Peter and St. Paul. Return to this point.

6.   Walk down the field to cross two stiles to reach Finkell Street. Turn right then left down Pitt Lane and at the end cross two stiles into a field. Follow a hawthorn hedge to cross a stile, then through a gate to reach a further road (Middlebridge Road). Turn right for a few metres then turn left past a barn. Over the stile and walk diagonally left across two fields to reach Wood Lane. Turn right, and walk down to reach the Chesterfield Canal again at Gringley Top Lock.

7.   Take the towpath along the canal by turning left and follow it for 3 km. Where the canal swings to the left you reach the Drakeholes Tunnel. Go up the slope and follow the path onto the road and down to the junction at the Griff Inn.

8.   Rejoin the canal opposite the Griff Inn and follow the towpath. Pass under Lady Bridge (note the bearded heads on both parapets) and continue to the next bridge: Taylor's Bridge (no. 71). We recommend you leave the canal at this point, turning right and walking into Wiseton. Turn left opposite two cottages (but take the opportunity to see Wiseton Hall) and pass Grange Farm to reach Wiseton Top Bridge). Turn right again and after 500 metres rejoin the canal and towpath. Go

along the towpath under Gray's Bridge and then Otter Bridge. Leave the canal at this point and retrace your steps back into Clayworth to return to your car on Church Lane.

POINTS OF INTEREST

Clayworth:

Church of St. Peter, which has a sundial over the porch at its entrance with the words *"Our days on the earth are as a shadow"*

Royston Manor:

The south front is said to date from 1588, but everything visible was rebuilt in 1891.

Beacon Hill is the site of a prehistoric fortress. Fine views are available from here, including Lincoln Cathedral and the Isle of Axeholme.

Wiseton:

The village has a late 18th century Wiseton Hall and stables as well as 18th and 19th century cottages across the road from the Hall gates.

Gringley on the Hill:

The village lies on the east spur of a range of hills lying in front of the Pennines, and offers wide views. The village clusters around the Church of St. Peter and St. Paul.

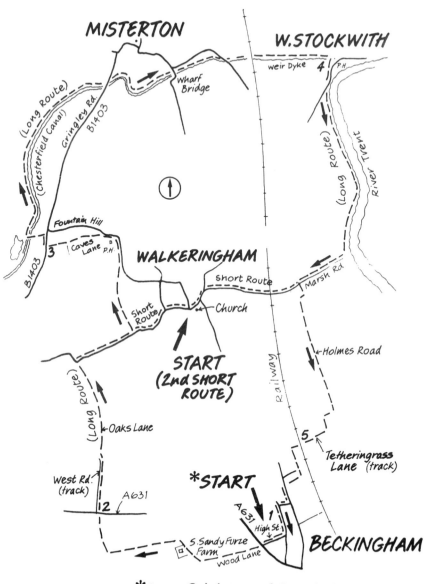

WALK 2

2. Walkeringham Wander

This walk can be tackled as one long route, or two short excursions.

THE FACTS

Area:	Beckingham, Walkeringham, Misterton, West Stockwith	
Distance:	Long route:	17 km (11 miles)
	Short routes:	8 km (5 miles) from Beckingham or 10 km (6 miles) from Walkeringham
Duration:	Long route:	5 hours
	Short routes:	2.5 - 3 hours
Maps Required:	OS Pathfinder 745 (SK 68/78) East Retford (North) & Blyth and 728 (SK 69/79) Harworth & Gringley on the Hill	
	OS Landranger 112 Scunthorpe	
Bus/Train Link:	Gainsborough	
Terrain:	Flat, mostly well-marked paths, some green lanes and tracks	
Starting Point:	Long & First short routes: Beckingham Village Green SK 781899	
	Second short route: Walkeringham SK 766924	
Refreshments:	Hare & Hounds, Beckingham; Brickmakers' Arms, Walkeringham; Packet Inn, Misterton; The Waterside Inn, West Stockwith. Other public houses are available just off the route.	

THE ROUTE

1.   From the Green, walk along High Street past the school following the road round to the right past the Village Institute. After the Methodist Church, turn left onto a cinder road (Ravensbeck Lane). Cross the A631 dual carriageway, where

there are strawberries for sale in season, and follow the footpath sign across the footbridge. The footpath crosses a muddy field. Continue in the same direction along Wood Lane until a signpost indicates a footpath through South Sandy Furze farmyard. Cross two and a half fields to a footpath T-junction. Turn right across the field to the A631.

2.   In just over 600 metres a signposted path on the left crosses two fields, then follows a green lane and Westmoor Road ahead into Walkeringham. At North Moor Lane turn left, then left again into Cave's Lane just before the Brickmaker's Arms.

Short Route: Start at the footpath on Gringley Road, (see map) walk on past the Church to meet Beckingham Road on the edge of Walkeringham village. Turn left after the village cross, then right down Station Road. You then continue the walk from Paragraph 4, where you turn right to walk down Holmes Road.

3.   Make a right turn along the B1403 at Fountain Hill, **taking care** as there is no pavement. On the left is the old brickworks, take the lane that leads to it. Go over Smith's Bridge and drop down to join the Chesterfield Canal towpath to the right to Misterton. The Packet Inn on the canal side has benches outside but does not open most weekday lunchtimes in winter.

4.   Continue on the towpath until the Canal joins the River Trent at West Stockwith. Boating enthusiasts may wish to look round the basin. The route crosses the road half-right at Basin Bridge with the Waterside Inn on the left. Walk past the Yacht Club to the riverside. Turn right to rejoin the road and take the path on the left that follows the bank of the River Trent in a southerly direction. At Point Farm, cross the stile onto Marsh Road to the second track on the left (Holmes Road). Turn left *(or right if you are joining from the short route)* and continue down Holmes Road past Holmes Villas to take a right turn, then a left turn to join Tetheringrass Lane.

5.   Turn right along this lane and go over the railway line. At the road junction in Beckingham turn left along Low Street, then right up Church Street. Go through the kissing gate into the churchyard and follow the footpath from the corner of the churchyard to the Green in Beckingham.

The second short route starts at the Brickmaker's Arms, Walkeringham, following the route from paragraph 2 up Fountain Hill Road, Cave's Lane, along the Canal towpath and by the river until you reach the junction of Marsh Road and Holmes Road, where the first short route rejoined. You then walk back along the route described for the first short alternative, along Station Road, past the cross and the church and into Walkeringham village.

POINTS OF INTEREST

Beckingham:
All Saints Church dates from the 13th century.

Walkeringham:
St. Mary Magdalen Church, with a monument to Francis Williamson, who died in 1639, and his wife portrayed as two life-size figures with their three kneeling children.

The Manor House stands beside the Church on the main road.

Misterton:
All Saints Church, Methodist Church dating from 1878, ancient farms dating back to 1600.

Canal Basin where the River Trent meets the Chesterfield Canal at West Stockwith

West Stockwith:
St. Mary's Church was built in 1722.

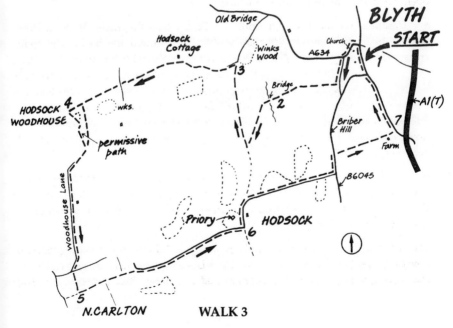

WALK 3

3. Ancient Churches Of North Nottinghamshire

An interesting ramble taking in some lovely old churches and a priory.

THE FACTS

Area:	Blyth, Carlton in Lindrick, Hodsock Priory
Distance:	11 km (7 miles)
Duration:	3.5 - 4 hours
Maps Required:	OS Pathfinder 744 (SK 48/58) Aughton & Carlton in Lindrick and 745 (SK 68/78) East Retford (North) and Blyth
	OS Landranger 120 Mansfield & Worksop
Bus/Train Link:	Worksop
Terrain:	Mostly well-marked, level paths and tracks. Suitable for dogs, except in Hodsock Priory if you are intending to visit. A good winter walk.
Starting Point:	White Swan, Blyth SK 624871
Refreshments:	Public house in North Carlton

THE ROUTE

1.   From the White Swan walk towards the church. Cross the road and turn left on the A634 Rotherham Road (note village sign - see notice board outside White Swan for full details). Pass the houses and as the road bears right, take the path to the left along a track. You are now entering Blyth Park. After 200 metres take a path to the right downhill and pass through a gate into a narrow field. Cross diagonally to the left, over a stile and straight ahead along the field side to a bridge (River Ryton).

2. Cross the bridge and proceed through a small wood to the corner of a field. Straight on again along the field edge to a gap (don't miss it!), then diagonally left across the next field towards the opposite corner. Sharp right and continue along the top edge of two fields to a gap in the hedge. Continue through rough scrub until reaching a small tarmac road. Turn left.

3. Carry on along the lane past several buildings on the right, then uphill ignoring the footpath to the left and after 500 metres cross over a path junction.

4. As the road bears right, take the left hand path which passes between two houses (Hodsock Woodhouse), **this is a permissive route**, the footpath is just past the wood then right past a house, bear left over a small stream and straight on uphill across a field to a stile in the hedge. Turn right onto Woodhouse Lane and continue for 1.5 km to a T-junction. Turn right and in 150 metres left, then in 20 metres right onto a field path for 250 metres, and a path junction (Carlton lies 300 metres to the right).

5. At the junction take the left path which meets another, turn left over a stile, and cross three fields, then right on to a gravel lane. Pass through Hodsock Priory buildings with the Priory on the left. Bear left past Priory Farm, onto the driveway.

6. Carry on to the end of the driveway to reach the Blyth/Worksop road at Briber Hill. Turn left and cross the road, then turn right towards Spital Farm, to reach Blyth and your start point.

POINTS OF INTEREST
Blyth:

The Norman Church of St. Mary and St. Martin (AD 1088) is definitely worth a visit, being the only remains of the priory. It has a wonderful Medieval Doom Painting of the Last Judgement which was whitewashed over and hidden for about 450 years. It was only rediscovered in 1985.

Also in Blyth is a 13th century Leper Hospital, later used as a village school, and in the Second World War employed as a canteen and rest room for soldiers. It is now converted to two dwellings.

Hodsock Priory is the home of Sir Andrew and Lady Buchanan. There was never a priory here, although the large moated manor house dated from 13th century. The grounds are frequently open to visitors (snowdrops in February daily; grounds open April to July, but not every day). No dogs.

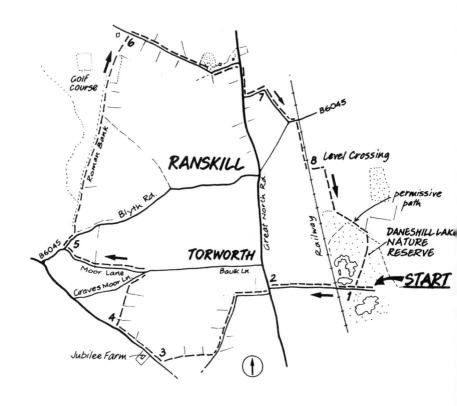

Golf course

Roman Bank

6

RANSKILL

7

B6045

8 Level Crossing

permissive path

DANESHILL LAKE NATURE RESERVE

Blyth Rd.

Great North Rd.

Railway

B6045

5

Moor Lane

TORWORTH

Baulk Ln.

2

START

1

Graves Moor Ln.

4

Jubilee Farm

3

WALK 4

4. The Roman Bank Of Ranskill

An easy walk starting at the Daneshill Lakes Nature Reserve, following country roads to join the ancient Roman embankment of Ranskill and the parklands of Serlby.

THE FACTS

Area:	Torworth and Ranskill
Distance:	12 km (7.5 miles)
Duration:	3.75 hoursMaps Required: OS Pathfinder 745 (SK 68/78) East Retford (North) & Blyth
	OS Landranger 120 Mansfield & Worksop
Bus/Train Link:	Retford
Terrain:	Easy walking, fairly flat
Starting Point:	Daneshill Nature Reserve Car Park SK 670865
Refreshments:	Public houses in Ranskill and Torworth

THE ROUTE

1.   Leave the car park and return along Daneshill Road to Torworth going over the railway crossing.

2.   At the Great North Road turn left, then immediate right along a narrow lane. Soon after passing a lone house on the right, turn right and follow a hedged lane for 500 metres to meet the A634.

3.   Turn right (A634) past Jubilee Farm and walk for 450 metres to reach a byway on the right.

4.   Follow the byway to reach Graves Moor Lane. Turn right and walk 200 metres

to Moor Lane on the left. Go along Moor Lane to reach the B6045 (Blyth Road).

5.   Turn right and walk 150 metres to reach Roman Bank Lane. Our path now follows this earthwork for 2 km and is a delightful route bordering the Serlby Park Golf Course.

6.   On reaching the road, turn right and walk 1.25 km to reach once again the Old Great North Road (A638).

7.   Turn right and walk to Folly Hook Lane on your left. Follow this as far as Mattersey Road. Turn left and just before the railway take a path on the right leading onto Station Road.

8.   Turn left over the railway crossing and after 200 metres turn right down a wide, sandy track. After 400 metres fork left for a further 400 metres and then turn right to follow a permissive path along a stream through the Nature Reserve and back to the car park. You now have the opportunity to have a stroll around the Nature Reserve.

POINTS OF INTEREST

Serlby Hall, a three-storey late Georgian house, was originally built for the Second Viscount Galway in 1750 by James Paine. It stands high up on a ridge above the River Ryton.

Daneshill Lake Nature Reserve has been owned by Nottinghamshire County Council since 1982. The one-time gravel workings have now been allowed to regenerate naturally covering an area of 120 acres with a wide variety of plant, animal and bird life. There are opportunities for bird-watching, water sports and walking.

5. Wheatley's Green Lanes and Towpaths

One of three walks from North Wheatley, this one linking the village of Clayworth, then going down the Chesterfield Canal past the Clayworth Boatyard to the village of Hayton, then over the hill with excellent views back to North Wheatley.

THE FACTS

Area:	North Wheatley, Clayworth, Hayton
Distance:	11 km (7 miles)
Duration:	3.5 hours
Maps Required:	OS Pathfinder 745 (SK 68/78) East Retford (North) & Blyth
	OS Landranger 120 Mansfield & Worksop
Bus/Train Link:	Retford
Terrain:	Tracks, green lanes, field paths and towpaths
Starting Point:	Sun Inn, North Wheatley SK 756859 Park at the side of the lane running past the Sun Inn
Refreshments:	Sun Inn, North Wheatley; Brewers Arms public house, Clayworth; Boat Inn, Hayton

THE ROUTE

1. Pass the Sun Inn on your right and then turn left towards the A620 dual carriageway, taking the road to Clayworth. After 440 metres you will see a track on your right: Northfield Leys Road.

2. Follow this track for almost 1.8 km, then turn left along the edge of a field.

13

After 200 metres turn right along a green lane, and after about 250 metres turn left at the cross roads into Mill Lane, heading to Clayworth.

3.   At the junction with Toft Dyke Lane, turn left, still on Mill Lane, and follow the road into the village. *If at this point you are in need of refreshment, turn right and you will see the Brewers Arms public house on your right after about 100 metres.* Otherwise, turn left, keeping to the main road for 440 metres until you reach the bridge over the canal.

4.   At this point, cross the bridge and join the towpath on your left and walk along the Canal towards Hayton. You will pass through the Clayworth Boatyard where there is usually a good selection of modern and traditional narrow boats on view. Follow the towpath for almost 3.5 km.

5.   When you reach Hayton you will see the Boat Inn, where you rejoin the road, cross Townsend Bridge and turn left and then immediately right, climbing up Hollinhill Lane. After 300 metres at the cross roads with Cordall Lane, continue straight on.

6.   After a further 880 metres, at the T-junction with Hangingside Lane, go over a stile which is slightly offset and to the right. Follow the track for about 300 metres then go over another stile.

7.   Follow a similar line across the field keeping the distant power station to your right. When you reach the field edge path at the other side of the field, turn left for 50 metres then turn right and follow the field edge path until you reach the end of the field. Here you turn left and walk up the field edge.

8.   On reaching Middle Hill Road turn right and follow the track until it crosses the dual carriageway, and take the small lane opposite and return to the Sun Inn.

POINTS OF INTEREST

Chesterfield Canal Towpath:

Along this stretch of the towpath it is quite common to see herons amongst many other species of birds.

North Wheatley:

The church of St. Peter and St. Paul was much restored in the nineteenth centuries, but remnants of the Medieval church still remain in the top windows.

Manor House, Low Street, dated 1673 with Cartwright arms in a panel above the door.

Numerous dovecotes in the village, nearly every sizeable farm has one either as a separate building or above farm buildings.

Clayworth:

Church of St. Peter, which has a sundial over the porch at its entrance with the words *"Our days on the earth are as a shadow"*.

The village stands on an old Roman road running north-east from East Retford.

Hayton:

Church of St. Peter, the oldest parts of which are late 12th century, with a 14th century font.

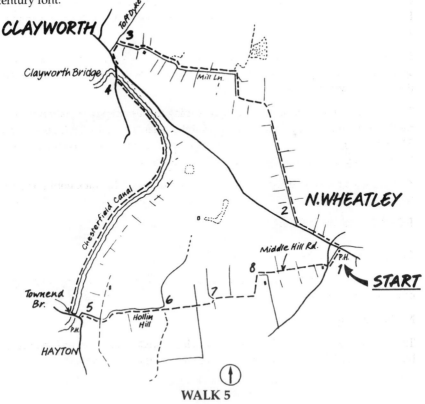

WALK 5

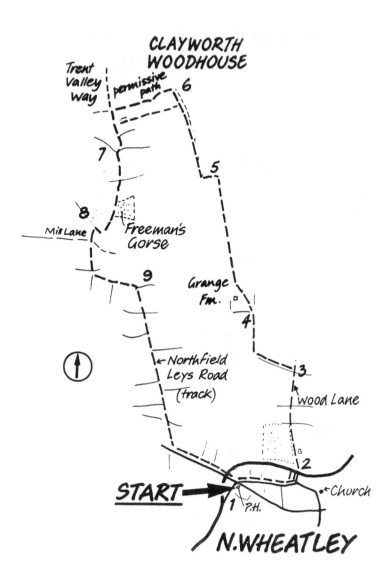

CLAYWORTH
WOODHOUSE

Trent
Valley
Way

permissive
path

6

7

5

8

Mill Lane

Freeman's
Gorse

9

Grange
Fm.

4

←Northfield
Leys Road
(track)

3

Wood Lane

2

START →

1 P.H.

•←Church

N.WHEATLEY

WALK 6

6. North Nottinghamshire's Lost Village

The second of three walks from North Wheatley, this going across to the former village settlement of Clayworth Woodhouse, returning along Hangman's Lane and the Trent Valley Way with excellent views of the surrounding countryside.

THE FACTS

Area:	North Wheatley, Clayworth Woodhouse
Distance:	9 km (5.5 miles)
Duration:	2.5 - 3 hours
Maps Required:	OS Pathfinder 745 (SK 68/78) East Retford (North) & Blyth
	Landranger 112 Scunthorpe
Bus/Train Link:	Retford
Terrain:	Tracks, green lanes, field paths and metalled roads
Starting Point:	Sun Inn, North Wheatley SK 756859 Park at the side of the lane running past the Sun Inn
Refreshments:	Sun Inn, North Wheatley
Please note:	**In paragraph 5 we describe the definitive line of the footpath. However, because the path is difficult to walk, we also describe a permissive route as an alternative. We shall be endeavouring to have the definitive line properly reinstated.**

THE ROUTE

1. With the Sun Inn on your right-hand side, cross the road and take Top Street

for 500 metres. After passing the Old Plough guest house, take the second turning on the left.

2.   At the dual-carriageway cross over and take Wood Lane which is almost immediately opposite. *Just up this lane, fresh fruit may be purchased in season.* Follow this lane for 1.3 km through open agricultural land and the occasional strawberry field, until you reach a crossroads.

3.   At the crossroads turn left towards Wheatley Grange Farm. After 400 metres, turn right just before the cattle grid and gate to Wheatley Grange Farm, through a hole in the hedge and keep to the right-hand side of the hedge. *Look out for rabbits scampering within the thick hedge.*

4.   At the brow of a slight rise you will see a sizeable gap in the hedge. Turn approximately 45° left and aim to the top diagonal corner of the field. At the top of the field bear right and follow the field edge.

5.   After just over 440 metres you will reach a hedge crossing at right angles. Turn left for 150 metres, then turn right at the next hedge. You will now see the ancient settlement of Clayworth Woodhouse directly in front of you. Follow the footpath to the boundary on the left side of farm buildings at Clayworth Woodhouse. To follow the **definitive line** go ahead to the fence, then turn left on the undefined footpath, across two fields to Hangman's Lane.

6.   If the crossfield path should be obstructed, then follow the **permissive path** as follows. Pass left of the fenced enclosure at Clayworth Woodhouse to a stile, then continue to another stile beside the stable. Turn left along the field edge path to a wide grassy area, and cross the stile to a further stile on the left to reach Hangman's Lane. You now join the definitive path.

7.   You are now on one of Nottinghamshire's long distance footpaths: *The Trent Valley Way.* Turn left if on the definitive line, or straight on if on the **permissive route** to follow the field edge path to reach a small coppice. In 440 metres you will emerge from the coppice, continue along the hedge eventually reaching a cart track where you turn left.

8.   After 100 metres go over a slightly offset crossroads, keeping to the green lane, turning left after 250 metres and follow the hedge until you reach a track.

9.   Turn right along the track: this is Northfield Leys Road, for almost 1.8 km. At the end of this track you will meet a road, turn left and follow the road for 440

metres, then cross over the dual carriageway. The Sun Inn should now be immediately in front of you.

POINTS OF INTEREST

North Wheatley:

The Church of St. Peter and St. Paul. Much restored in the nineteenth centuries, but remnants of the Medieval church still remain in the top windows.

The Manor House on Low Street dates from 1673, with the Cartwright arms in a panel above the front door.

The village has numerous dovecotes, nearly every sizeable farm has one either in separate buildings or above farm buildings.

Clayworth Woodhouse:

The Church of St. Peter. There is a sundial over the porch to the church entrance with the words *"Our days on the earth are as a shadow"*.

Clayworth:

The village stands on an old Roman road running north-east from East Retford.

7. On The Saintly Path

The last of three circular walks going from North Wheatley, this one linking the ancient churches of The Wheatleys and Clarborough. This walk offers attractive walking and excellent views.

THE FACTS

Area:	North and South Wheatley, Clarborough
Distance:	10 km (6 miles)
Duration:	3 hours
Maps Required:	OS Pathfinder 745 (SK 68/78) East Retford (North) & Blyth
	Landranger 120 Mansfield & Worksop
Bus/Train Link:	Retford
Terrain:	Metalled roads, tracks and field paths
Starting Point:	Sun Inn, North Wheatley SK 756859 Park at the side of the lane running past the Sun Inn
Refreshments:	Sun Inn, North Wheatley; and with a short detour the King's Arms, Clarborough

THE ROUTE

1.   With the Sun Inn on your right-hand side, turn left down Low Street to the Church Hill/Sturton Road junction. Walk straight across along Lower Pasture Lane to take the footpath on the right which crosses the fields to the ruins of St. Helen's Church, South Wheatley. Turn right on the main road (Sturton Road) and walk 550 metres to a sharp bend. Take the lane on your left which is Muspit Lane.

2.   Continue along Muspit Lane for 2.2 km. The lane gradually peters out to a

footpath. Where it crosses Blue Stocking Lane, turn right for 50 metres, then turn left into Howbeck Lane towards Clarborough.

3.   At the top of Howbeck Lane enjoy the views of Nottinghamshire and South Yorkshire. At the junction, bear slightly right and continue to Clarborough.

4.   As you enter Clarborough, just before the first house turn right and go through the gate and along the footpath, over three stiles, then cross the A620 Retford/Gainsborough road and rejoin the green lane (Lovers' Walk) slightly offset to the right.

4a.   Alternatively, you may be in need of refreshment, in which case continue down Howbeck Lane until you reach the main A620. Turn right and after 200 metres you will find the King's Arms on your right. When you leave, turn right and follow the main road, turning right up the hill where you will see the green lane described in paragraph 4.

5.   After 500 metres tracks cross, turn right here into Hangingside Lane, going up the steep gradient. After a further 500 metres, turn right into Goit Lane, ignoring the footpath to your right. In the distance straight ahead can be seen West Burton Power Station. The lane has a right-angled bend and there is a climb uphill.

6.   At the top of the hill the lane finishes. Here turn right and keep a straight line across the field, keeping the distant power station on your right as you look ahead.

7.   When you reach the field edge path at the other side of the field, turn left for 50 metres, then right and follow the field edge path until you reach the end of the field. Here you turn left and walk up the field edge.

8.   At the end of the field edge path turn right along the track: this is Middle Hill Road. Follow the track until it crosses the dual carriageway and take the small lane opposite and return to the Sun Inn.

POINTS OF INTEREST

North Wheatley:

The Church of St. Peter and St. Paul. Much restored in the nineteenth centuries, but remnants of the Medieval church still remain in the top windows.

The Manor House on Low Street dates from 1673, with the Cartwright arms in a panel above the front door.

The village has numerous dovecotes, nearly every sizeable farm has one either in separate buildings or above farm buildings.

South Wheatley:

This village is almost joined to North Wheatley, and contains many interesting farm buildings and dovecotes, some of which date from the 18th century.

The small ruined 12th century Norman church of St. Helen's fell into disrepair in 1883. The only remains are the chancel arch and west tower, standing amongst thick clumps of elders.

Clarborough:

St. John the Baptist Church, with its octagonal font and eighteenth century monument.

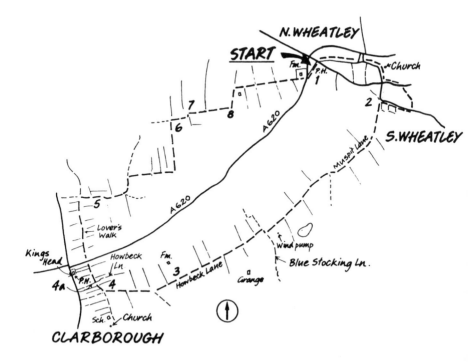

WALK 7

8. Ancient Churches, Wallingwells and a Stately Home That Never Was!

A walk starting in the beautiful and historic village of South Carlton, passes Wallingwells, a nunnery turned stately home, and the delightful Langold Country Park.

THE FACTS

Area:	South Carlton, Wallingwells, Langold Country Park
Distance:	14 km (8.5 miles)
Duration:	4 hours
Maps Required:	OS Pathfinder 744 (SK 48/58) Aughton & Carlton in Lindrick
	OS Landranger 120 Mansfield & Worksop
Bus/Train Link:	Worksop
Terrain:	Flat, can get boggy in woodland
Starting Point:	South Carlton Church SK 587839
Refreshments:	Grey Horses Inn, Blue Bell and Sherwood Ranger public houses, North Carlton

THE ROUTE

1.   With your back to the church, turn left and stroll down to the mill. Pass in front of the mill and go up a twitchell past Field House Farm, then choose the path going half-right. After the first field take the left of two signposted paths to reach Owday Lane just left of a lone house. Turn right, go round the first corner and straight on at the next through woodland. Next, turn right along a hedgeside farm track and when it turns left, keep straight on.

2.   Passing through a belt of trees, keep ahead across arable land to a gap in the

23

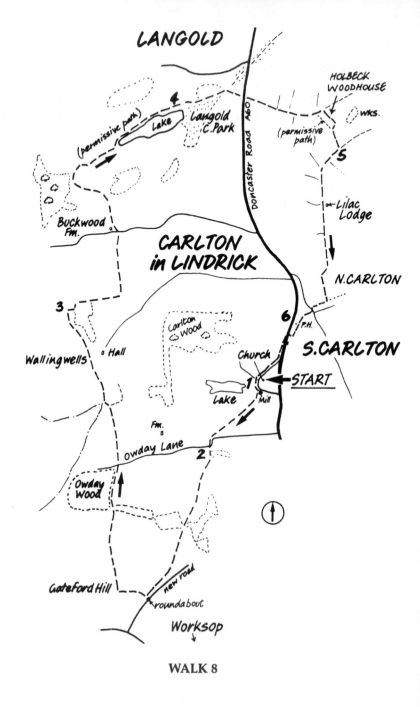

WALK 8

hedge. Development is taking place in this area, but a footpath is already marked out going right, parallel to a main road. At a roundabout, turn right and follow the road right again. The road becomes a farm lane and passes along the edge of Owday Wood. Cross Owday Lane again and follow the track, keeping left where the track bends right. The track passes close to Wallingwells, the former nunnery, and joins another track in a T-junction.

3.   Turn right and then left after 500 metres, go on to a road and cross it, passing Buckwood Farm. Follow the farm road which skirts the former pit-heap, cross a stile beside a farm gate and immediately a stile left. Follow a short field edge path then head half-right across arable land to Langold Holt. Do not cross the stream, but turn right along a wide field edge path beside the stream which widens into a lake. This is a permissive path going into Langold Country Park. Where the water tumbles over a weir, cross the causeway left and continue round the main lake.

4.   At the end of the lake turn left, then right just before the kiosk and pass right through the wood. Turn right across the grass, pass a brick building, go on to the A60 and cross it. After 900 metres turn right down the drive to Hodsock Woodhouse *(this is a permissive route, the footpath is right just past the wood, then right past a house)*. Go between the houses, over a footbridge and turn right on to the road.

5.   Follow the hedged lane to a T-junction, turn right and at the next junction cross the road to enter a sports field. Keep to the left hedge and edge into the remains of a hedged path, continuing across rough grassland. There are several paths, mostly unofficial, but keep right to the corner of the field and follow the twitchell to Greenway. Turn left, first right then left past the Grey Horses Inn. Follow this street right to the A60.

6.   The Blue Bell public house, to the right, serves meals. Our route is left, past the Sherwood Ranger and right after 400 metres to reach South Carlton Church.

POINTS OF INTEREST

Wallingwells:

This was a Benedictine priory of nuns founded in the reign of King Stephen to house 9 sisters and a prioress. The present hall dates from the late 16th century, when the estate was purchased by Sir Richard Pipe, a Lord Mayor of London.

Langold Country Park was created in the early 19th century for a stately home which was never completed. It was bought from the Coal Board in 1974 by Bassetlaw District Council.

Carlton in Lindrick:

This is actually two villages: South Carlton (Carlton Barron) and North Carlton (originally Kingston-in-Carlton). South Carlton was mentioned in the Domesday book and was probably a Saxon village with a church and mill. The Church of St. John the Evangelist, South Carlton has much Saxon masonry and houses the Becket Altar with four carved crosses and a lead sealed relic.

Outside the church door stands the Devil Stone', probably an old font, which according to local legend, brings ill fortune to those who try to put it to secular use. The other legend exhorts you to run around it seven times: you will either have good luck, or see the Devil!

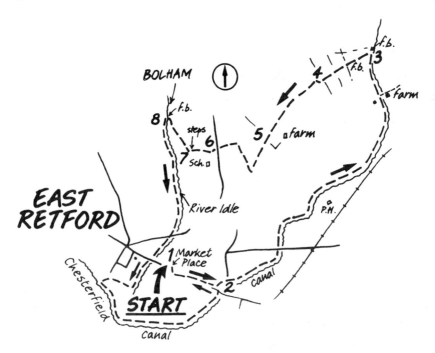

WALK 9

9. An Idle Walk Around Retford

An easy stroll along a busy section of the Chesterfield Canal then across the water meadows to link onto the River Idle floodbank back into Retford town centre.

THE FACTS

Area: Retford

Distance: 9 km (5.5 miles)

Duration: 2.5 hours

Maps Required: OS Pathfinder 745 (SK 68/78) East Retford (North) and Blyth

                 OS Landranger 120 Mansfield & Worksop

Bus/Train Link: Retford

Terrain: Towpaths, field paths and footways

Starting Point: Retford Market Place SK 709811

Refreshments: The Hop Pole or several public houses in Retford

THE ROUTE

1.   With your back to the Market Place walk down Grove Street crossing Arlington Way at the traffic lights and continuing straight on to reach the Chesterfield Canal.

2.   At the canal turn left and walk along the towpath for 3 km passing Grove Mill, now a snooker centre, Whitsunday Pie Lock, and a bridge marked 61 from Bonemill Farm.

3.   Some 360 metres from this bridge just before a footbridge (SK 720833) leave the towpath taking the path on the left. Cross the field aiming to the centre of the hedge seen ahead to reach a footbridge.

4.   Continue in the same direction across two further fields (hedge on the right).

Cross a ditchboard, then aim for a fingerpost 25 metres away on the right. Turn left over the ditchboard, then crossing a large field again aiming for a hedge seen ahead. After crossing a further ditchboard continue in the same direction until you reach Bigsby Road.

5.   Walk down Bigsby Road past Winston Grove to reach Cornwall Road. Turn down this to reach Palmer Road. Turn left and continue to Tiln Lane.

6.   Cross Tiln Lane aiming slightly to the left to walk down Carr Hill Way and River Close to reach some steps between houses nos. 20-22, onto Bolham Lane.

7.   Turn right and walk to the end of Bolham Lane to reach a footbridge over the River Idle.

8.   Cross the bridge, turn left and follow the river path back into Retford (1.75 km). *You will see East Retford and West Retford churches with the Retford Town Hall clock located between them.* After passing under the A620 roadbridge (Amcott Way) we leave the riverside to come onto the road at Bridgegate. Turn left and walk towards a roundabout. *This was the Great North Road.* 20 metres before the roundabout, turn right into the White Hart yard. *The White Hart was a coaching inn. Look through the watch shop window: these were the stables.* Leave by the other archway into the Market Square.

POINTS OF INTEREST
Retford:

The market town of East Retford and the village of West Retford stand on opposite banks of the River Idle. They are now entirely one.

The town received a Charter in 1246, and owed its Georgian prosperity to its position on the Great North Road diverted through it in 1766, and on the Chesterfield Canal which was opened in 1777.

Church of St. Swithin.

King Edward VI Grammar School on London Road, founded 1552.

Sloswicke's Hospital on Churchgate, founded 1657.

Chesterfield Canal:

Along this stretch of the towpath it is quite common to see herons amongst many other species of birds.

10. Trent Valley Windmill

The Green Lanes around North and South Leverton are a feature of this walk which includes North Leverton windmill, still a genuine working mill for the local community.

THE FACTS

Area: North Leverton, South Leverton

Distance: 12 km (7.5 miles) Duration: 3 hours

Maps Required: OS Pathfinder 745 (SK 68/78) East Retford

OS Landranger 120 Mansfield & Worksop

Bus/Train Link: Retford

Terrain: No steep climb, easy underfoot except after heavy rain. Fields paths and green lanes.

Starting Point: North Leverton Church SK 786822

Refreshments: The Plough public house, South Leverton; The Royal Oak public house, North Leverton

THE ROUTE

1.   From the entrance of North Leverton church on Main Street, head away from the village centre for 70 metres and take the path signposted to the right along the left-hand edge of a garden. Cross the stile at the end and continue across the grass field to a row of bushes where the field once ended. Turn left to a double fence, go on to the entrance to another field and cross the stile to your right.

2.   Continue with the hedge on your left, pass the poultry farm and go on as before. After crossing a footbridge, go a few metres right then left along the field edge path to join a green lane - Newings Lane. Keep ahead and follow the lane

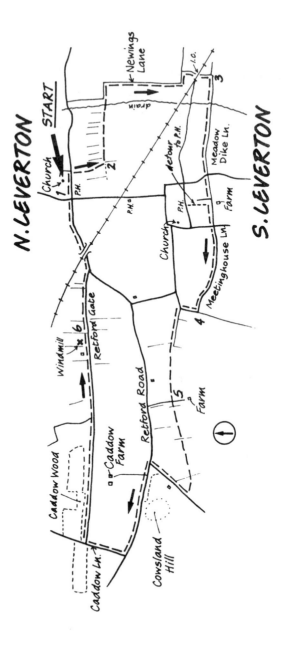

WALK 10

right, then left after 1 km. 100 metres on take the green lane on the right, cross a railway line **with care** and turn left along a road.

3.   Only 100 metres on, turn left into Meadow Dike Lane which has a good firm surface. At a crossroads, cross Rampton Lane and go on to Brickings Lane and High Street, South Leverton. *For a detour to the public house, turn right before the first house, follow the twitchell to the end and turn left. If you do this, you must turn left and first right to rejoin the route.*

Otherwise go straight on across Church Street into Meeting House Lane. After a double bend, this goes out of the village.

4.   At a T-junction, turn right on Millfield Road, then left as signposted on the next bend. This is Hollowgate Road, another green lane. The path goes straight on at the end to a stile and footbridge, past a pond and along the wide field edge path at the edge of a large field. Near the top, cross a plank bridge on the right and continue up hill.

5.   Across an access road, go a few metres right to a stile and resume the uphill path at the right-hand edge of a grass and arable field. In the last arable field you go ahead to the signposted stile. Follow the road to the right and at the end turn left up the Retford Road until you reach Caddow Lane to the right. Follow this green lane only as far as Retford Gate, a wide track on your right which after 2 km reaches North Leverton Windmill.

6.   Pass the Mill and continue down Mill Lane and along the pavement into North Leverton. Your starting point is straight ahead.

POINTS OF INTEREST

South Leverton:

The village has many traditional Nottinghamshire red brick buildings of particular note, with a late 17th century dovecote and the Church of All Saints, which has a fine Norman tower. The first house in Meeting House Lane is Quaker Cottage, so called because it was given to the Quakers in 1650 as a place for them to meet.

The Priory was built in 1166 of locally-quarried stone and is historically connected to the church.

31

North Leverton:

At the crossroads in the village are some of the finest farm buildings dating from the early 19th century. The church of St. Martin dates from the 12th century. There is an 18th century dovecote in the High Street. *North Leverton Windmill* was a subscription mill, built in 1813 by and for farmers in the local parishes to grind corn. It is now a limited company, but still processes grain for animal feed.

11. The Cavaliers of Castle Hill

After following the Chesterfield Canal into the heart of Retford, the walk climbs very gradually to the ridge above the Trent Valley and returns to a spectacular view over Little Gringley and the Idle Valley.

THE FACTS

Area:	East Retford, Little Gringley
Distance:	11 km (7 miles)
Duration:	3.5 hours
Maps Required:	OS Pathfinder 745 (SK 68/78) East Retford & Blyth
	OS Landranger 120 Mansfield & Worksop
Bus/Train Link:	Retford
Terrain:	Mostly easy, but some muddy areas
Starting Point:	Lay-by near the Hop Pole Inn, Retford SK 718818
Refreshments:	Hop Pole and Packet Inn, Retford

THE ROUTE

1.   From the lay-by near the Hop Pole Inn, walk towards East Retford, pass the pub to the bridge over the Chesterfield Canal, then cross the road to reach the towpath. Turn right and follow the canal to Grove Mill, then cross the bridge past the Packet Inn. Turn right immediately along a narrow lane, and at the end keep left along Pennington Walk. Cross Trent Street and follow Holly Lane to a railway bridge.

2.   Go on to a street, 25 metres left, then right as signposted along a twitchell. Cross a stile at the end and go straight ahead. After another stile, the path is nearly straight to Bracken Lane in grass fields, though the stiles tend to be in muddy

33

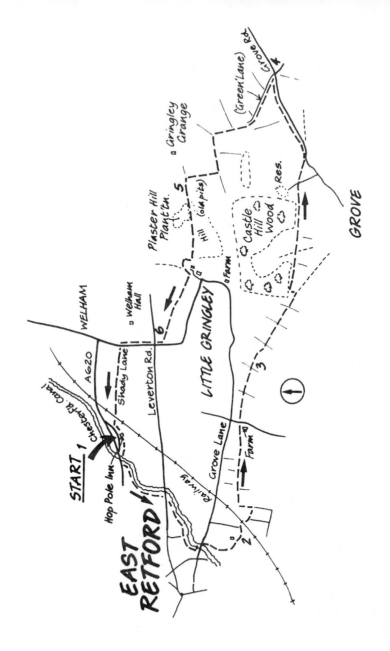

WALK 11

corners. Cross the lane and follow the left-hand hedge, still in grass fields, and straight ahead in the second field to the left corner.

3.   After passing a gateway on the left you will find a stile and footbridge, then go up the hill with the hedge now on your right. After the second field, turn left to walk beside Swindell Spring Wood and after a stile, keep ahead to follow the edge of Castle Hill Wood. After a stile, go ahead along a field edge path to join a tarmac drive, then cross the stile left and angle across the field to a road. As you follow this left, there is a view over the Trent Valley, dominated by three power stations. Go as far as a green lane on the left just before a road junction.

4.   Entering a field after 1 km, turn left along the headland, then along the second side. Go ahead over a plank bridge, but tread carefully as there is a pothole nearby. Now follow the hedge left to a stile, and walk along a small grass field to pass left of a wood. The view from here over Little Gringley and Retford beyond makes your exertions well worth while!

5.   From here the path angles right to join a hedge which leads to Little Gringley. After crossing a stile, follow a very angular route, first right up the paddock, then left along the top, then down a bit to a stile. Climb down into the green lane and keep left as far as the gate to Pond Farm. Here, unfortunately, you go through the gate opposite into an enclosure used for horses and extremely muddy, especially in the gateway opposite. However, you next go down the grass field to a stile near the right corner, then turn left in another grass field to a road, unloading the mud as you go !

6.   Turn right along the lane, cross the Leverton Road and continue to Welham along Little Gringley Lane. On the left you will find Shady Lane, a delightful path which takes you back to your starting point.

POINTS OF INTEREST

Grove Hall situated in the village of the same name is a white stuccoed house built in 1762 by John Carr. Grove was also the one-time home of the Grove Hunt'.

During the Civil War a skirmish alledgedly took place between **Castle Hill Wood** and **Swindell Spring Wood**, and even today there are local sightings of a Cavalier astride a white horse!

Retford:

The market town of East Retford and the village of West Retford stand on opposite banks of the river Idle, and are now entirely one.

The church of St. Swithun in East Retford stands in a large churchyard near the Market Place.

The town received its Charter in 1246, but owes its Georgian prosperity to its position on the Great North Road which was diverted through Retford in 1766, and on the Chesterfield Canal, which was opened in 1777.

12. Pilgrim Fathers' Walk

A circular walk starting from Retford linking the Chesterfield Canal to Babworth Church with its associations with the Pilgrim Fathers, then returning to Retford.

THE FACTS

Area:	Retford, Babworth
Distance:	14 km (9 miles)
Duration:	4 hours
Maps Required:	OS Pathfinder 745 (SK 68/78) East Retford (North) & Blyth and 763 (SK 67/77) Clumber Park and East Markham
	OS Landranger 120 Mansfield & Worksop
Bus/Train Link:	Retford
Terrain:	Towpaths, green lanes and woodland paths
Starting Point:	Retford Market Place SK 706813
Refreshments:	None en route. Plenty of facilities in Retford.

THE ROUTE

1.   From the Market Place walk in a southerly direction down Carolgate. Turn right after 200 metres along West Street crossing over the River Idle, then through King's Park to reach the Chesterfield Canal.

2.   Drop down right to join the towpath of the Canal. We now follow this towpath for 5 km passing a series of four locks known locally as Sherwood Forest Locks (they used to be inside the boundary of the Royal Forest of Sherwood). On reaching the fourth lock, we leave the Canal at the next bridge, with the number 52 on it.

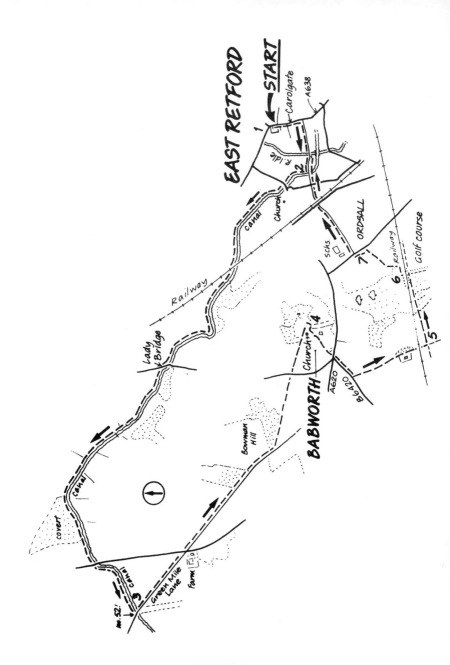

WALK 12

3. Go over the bridge and walk down Green Mile Lane, going over the old London Road and continuing to Bowman Hill Wood on the left side with New Plantation on the right. Take the path on the left and follow a clear route towards Babworth Church, keeping to the left of the tree clumps, and going over Sutton Lane to enter Babworth Park and our objective of Babworth Church. Take a well-earned rest and look around.

4. On leaving the church, follow the drive down to the main road, passing the old Vicarage (now called Haygarth Hall) to reach a major road junction. Cross the A620 and walk down Mansfield Road B6420. Follow the roadside path to reach a bridleway on the left in 300 metres. Follow the surfaced bridleway to Great Morton Farm and shortly after passing the farm take the underpass under the railway.

5. Turn left and walk parallel to the railway going through woodlands and across Retford Golf Course. **Take care not to disturb the golfers by keeping to the edge of the fairway: make sure they are aware of your presence.** Continue until you reach a bridge over the railway on your left.

6. Cross the railway, then turn right to the end of the wood, then left along a track to take a half-right line across a playing field to the right-hand corner to reach Ordsall Road.

7. Turn left for 100 metres, then take a right turn down Ordsall Park Road. After crossing the East Coast railway over the footbridge, walk straight ahead and then go down Pelham Road. Continue ahead on the bridge over the canal into King's Park. We now retrace our route back to the car park.

POINTS OF INTEREST

Pilgrim Fathers:

120 colonists left Plymouth in August 1620 in the "Mayflower" to settle the New World - America. These settlers: The Pilgrim Fathers originated in Nottinghamshire, in the villages of Scrooby and Babworth, which were centres of the Non-Conformist Movement during that time. There is a permanent Pilgrim Fathers Exhibition at Worksop Library and Museum, off Memorial Avenue.

Babworth:

The church of All Saints was heavily restored in the 19th century and contains monuments to the Simpson family.

Retford:

The market town of east Retford and the village of West Retford stand on opposite banks of the river Idle, and are now entirely one unit. The town received a charter in 1246, and owed its Georgian prosperity to its position on the Great North Road, which was diverted through it in 1766, and on the Chesterfield Canal, which was opened in 1777. The final achievement was the arrival of the railway from 1849.

The parish church is dedicated to St. Swithin. The King Edward VI Grammar School on London Road was founded in 1552.

13. Mines, Meadows and a Mill

A ramble through a well-wooded part of Nottinghamshire right on the Derbyshire border. As in much of the coal country, the mines have little impact on the delightful countryside and the paths are all well used.

THE FACTS

Area:	Langwith Mill, Warsop Vale, Church Warsop
Distance:	13 km (8 miles)
Duration:	4 hours
Maps Required:	OS Pathfinder 779 (SK 46/56) Mansfield (North) & Part of Sherwood Forest and OS 762 (SK 47/57) Staveley & Worksop (South)
	OS Landranger 120 Mansfield & Worksop
Bus/Train Link:	Worksop
Terrain:	Gently rolling, wooded. Woodland paths can become soggy after rain.
Starting Point:	Lay-by beside Langwith Mill SK 546701
Refreshments:	Jug & Glass public house, Nether Langwith; Vale Hotel, Warsop Vale

THE ROUTE

1.   From the end of the lay-by turn left down the lane past the Mill and Pasture Hill Farm and continue along the lane to the end and along the edge of the next field. Enter a meadow and cross it diagonally to the opposite corner. Enter the hedged lane, and at the end turn left.

2.   Where this farm road swings left to Blue Barn Farm, pass through the kissing-

41

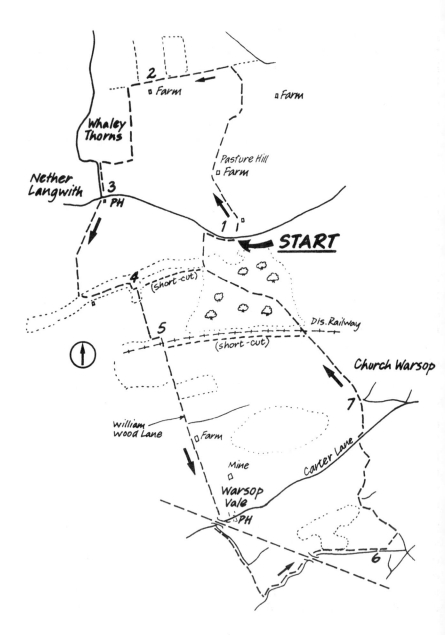

2

Farm

Farm

Whaley
Thorns

Pasture Hill
Farm

Nether
Langwith

3

PH

1

START

4

(short-cut)

5

Dis. Railway

(short-cut)

Church Warsop

7

William
Wood Lane

Farm

Carter Lane

Mine

Warsop
Vale

PH

6

WALK 13

gate ahead, go to the end of the meadow and left up the hill to join a lane. Follow this to a road and turn left to the main road at Nether Langwith. You may pass the Jug and Glass public house, but its setting, facing a green crossing by the tiny River Poulter, is very tempting!

3.   Cross the A632 and follow a hedged lane to the top of the hill with Top Farm in view. Turn left to a stile and follow a woodside path, turning right as the wood does, then left through it. At this point you may shorten the walk by going ahead and turning left in Cuckney Hay Wood.

4.   Our route turns right over a stile and along the edge of three fields. Turn left along the woodside for 50 metres, then right to climb stone steps to a disused railway track (again the walk can be shortened by following it left to a road.)

5.   Cross the track and follow the lane ahead which passes through the site of Warsop Main Colliery. On reaching the sharp left-hand bend, go straight on to the right of a row of cottages to Carter Lane, beside the Vale Hotel. Turn right under the railway bridge, then immediately left on a broad farm track, and where it turns left continue ahead in a delightful hedged path to Herrings Farm. *By turning right a short diversion can be made to visit Sookholme with its tiny Norman chapel in a field. Please retrace your steps to Herrings Farm.* We turn left (or go straight on if you walked into Sookholme) to walk along a stoney lane, under the railway again and across the river Meden.

At this point it is proposed to create a link with Stonebridge by walking along the Meden Trail. However, until this is established, please walk the route described above.

6.   We in the meantime continue along Sookholme Lane and on the fringe of Warsop take the first street (The Hawthorns) left, then left again along Stonebridge Lane. Cross the bridge over the Meden, *which isn't stone at all!* and continue through the Hills and Holes, the remains of a shallow limestone quarry now reclaimed by nature. Ignore a path on the left and continue in a green lane to Carter Lane. Go right for 50 metres and left up a fenced path to Church Warsop Miners' Welfare.

7.   Turn left along the road. Unfortunately the path parallel to the road in the wood to the left is unofficial, but it is well-walked. Pass the abutments of a dismantled bridge, ignore the first track left and continue a few metres to the corner of Cuckney Hay Wood. Here take the diagonal path through the wood, ignoring all side-tracks. At the far corner take the path downhill which leads out of the wood and along a hedged path to the A632. Turn right to return to the start.

POINTS OF INTEREST

Langwith Cotton Mill, built in 1760, was powered by the River Poulter. Nowadays, however, the mill house is a restaurant.

Whilst the walk takes in some limestone countryside, the whole area has been influenced by coalmining. However, sympathetic reclamation, together with existing woodland, has transformed this part of the Nottinghamshire/Derbyshire border.

Warsop:

This large parish includes several settlements. Warsop Vale was built after 1900 to house miners at Warsop Main Colliery. Spion Kop was established during the Boer War, and Welbeck Colliery Village and a mining community added to Church Warsop as the pits expanded. Shallow quarrying for Warsop lime has produced areas of humpy ground called Hills and Hollows, noted for birds and wild flowers.

The church of St. Peter and St. Paul at Church Warsop dates in parts from Norman times.

Also dedicated to St. Peter and St. Paul is the aisleless Norman chapel at Sookholme, again dating from around 1100.

Nether Langwith:

One of the barns at Langwith Mill Farm was an early water-powered cotton mill, dating from around 1780. It was large for its time, having four storeys and sixteen windows width. Upper Langwith, with the church, stands in Derbyshire.

14. An Archaeological Amble

Starting at one of the oldest known inhabited places in Britain, with numerous caves and a lovely limestone gorge, our walk also crosses one of the most beautiful Dukeries estates, crossing the county into Whitwell to return to Creswell.

THE FACTS

Area: Creswell Crags, Welbeck Abbey, Whitwell

Distance: 14 km (8.5 miles)

Duration: 4 hours

Maps Required: OS Pathfinder 762 (SK 47/57) Worksop (South) & Staveley and 763 (SK 67/77) Clumber Park and East Markham

OS Landranger 120 Mansfield & Worksop

Terrain: Field paths, country estate: an easy, varied walk

Starting Point: Visitors' Centre, Creswell Crags SK 538744 (**Note**: check on the closing time of the car park before commencing the walk)

Refreshments: Public houses in Whitwell

Nearest Town: Worksop

THE ROUTE

1.   After visiting the Visitors' Centre, take the wide track leading away from the main road and past the car park, through woods to meet the main A60.

2.   Cross the A60 and take the metalled road opposite, with a bridleway sign. This road is lined with conifers.

3.   At a T-junction near a lodge, go half-left along a concrete road going slightly uphill. At the top of the rise bear right and head towards a plantation taking no side turnings. The large building to the right was the Duke's Riding School.

4.   Just before reaching the plantation, cross a cattle grid and turn left along a

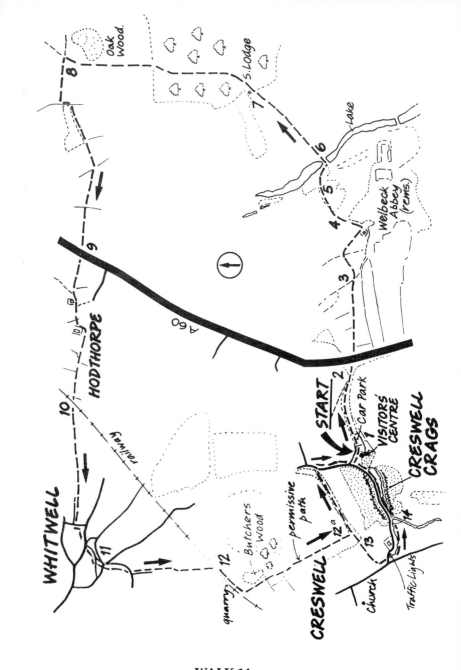

WALK 14

grassy track with a fence on the left. Go through a gate and continue around the outside of the plantation, then descend to a hand-gate in the corner of the field. The roofs now visible to the right are those of Welbeck Abbey.

5.   Go through the gate, bear right and continue to join a tarmac track. Turn right and go for a few metres to a junction, turn left and after 100 metres, left again, over the end of the Great Lake of Welbeck.

6.   Across the next field is a line of rough land. This marks the line of the Welbeck Tunnel. Walk parallel and just to the right of it. The line of the tunnel is marked by circular depressions in the ground, which are skylights to light and ventilate the tunnel. Most of the them are capped with concrete, but some are not, so whilst it is possible to go right up to them, care should be taken. Having followed this line across the field, you come into sight of a battlemented lodge (South Lodge). Just round the back of this lodge is the entrance to the tunnel, but this is boarded up and not very imposing.

7.   As you approach the lodge, at the edge of the small plantation on the left is a bridleway sign. Go through a hand gate into the plantation, then turn right along the side of a wooden fence to another hand gate. Turn left past an iron gateway towards the lodge. Do not take the path to the right, but walk to the rear of the lodge to take the footpath through a gate signposted 'Worksop 2 miles'. We continue along what is known as Tunnel Road through woods towards Worksop Manor soon seen in the distance.

8.   At the junction to the west of Castle Farm, turn left along a green lane signposted Whitwell and at the end turn left again to cross over a stile and go to the end of a wood. Turn right over a stream, then along the edge of a wood to go along a farm track. At the top of high ground after passing a gate on the right then walk diagonally across the field to reach a farm track and ditchboard to eventually reach the A60 (Worksop/Mansfield Road).

9.   Cross the road with care and enter a field walking towards electricity pole and buildings. Go over the stile going onto a farm track, and turn left to pass Binks Cottages. At the junction go over a fence, then along a track to a farm lane. Walk away from the farm and at the next junction turn right to go over the stile into a field. Cross to a further stile, and with the hedge on the right continue over the stile to a paddock next to the railway.

10. Cross over the railway and take the path across a field into Whitwell, aiming

for the left of a row of terraced bungalows. On reaching the end of Mill Lane, continue to its end, turn left down Hanger Hill, then right at the Main Street. *(Refreshments are available at several public houses and shops in the village.)*

11.   From the Medieval cross road junction, leave Whitwell by going up the steep Portland Street onto Titchfield Street and Bakestone Moor. Turn left down Franklin Avenue, and continue to the end to follow a footpath signposted Creswell. Follow the hedge and at its end where it meets a stone wall, turn right across the field to a hedge corner. Turn left with the hedge on the right and walk towards the quarry.

12.   On reaching the quarry, turn right along a descending footpath with the quarry embankment on your left and the railway cutting on your right. When the path descends to the level of the railway, turn left along the field edge path with the embankment of the quarry still to your left. Go forward to and through a stone wall to take a permissive footpath through a delightful narrow strip of trees. At the end of the road you join a sunken green lane. (At this point you have two choices, a quick route back to the Visitors' Centre along a delightful green lane by going left, or by going right to drop down into Creswell then to walk through the Creswell Gorge, which is something not to be missed.)

12a. If following the quick route, turn left along a green lane to reach the road. Turn right and return to the Visitors' Centre.

13.   To follow the longer route, turn right and drop downhill into Creswell. Turn left and walk to a road junction. Turn left, walking along the road. On reaching the traffic lights turn right to take a footpath to the stream, which you go over. Turn left and continue, keeping the stream to your left to the far end of a small lake and a T-junction. You are now walking along a Prehistoric Trail with caves along both sides of the limestone gorge!

14.   Turn left and proceed to the edge of the road, then turn sharp right and go down a path through a small wood to reach Creswell Crags Visitors' Centre and car park.

POINTS OF INTEREST

Creswell Crags:

This is one of the earliest known sites of man's occupation. A must is to make a visit to the Visitors Centre where Exhibitions and a vast wealth of information is to be found.

Welbeck Abbey:

Originally a Premonstratensian house founded in 1153-4, the estate passed into private hands after the Dissolution of the monasteries, and Welbeck became the country seat of the Dukes of Portland. Much of what exists today was created during a major building programme between 1854 and 1879, including the riding school and the three mile long tunnels.

The most enigmatic owner was the fifth Duke of Portland, who apparently lived in only four or five rooms, separated from the outside world by a door with two letter-boxes - one for messages and mail in, one out. He was friendly with the hundreds of workmen employed on his vast and crazy enterprises (although the local vicar had instructions not to see him if he passed in the park!), and each workman received a donkey and an umbrella when he started work so as to make travelling through the park more comfortable. One of the tunnels was constructed to convey the Duke to Worksop safe and unseen whenever the journey could not be avoided. It is still debated whether the tunnels were constructed to avoid spoiling the views above ground, or to indulge the Duke's morbid shyness.

Worksop Manor:

Built by the Earls of Shrewsbury, it passed by marriage to the Dukes of Norfolk who modernised and made further alterations. However, it was burnt down in 1761 and replaced by a splendid country house. However, in 1839 the estate was sold to the Duke of Newcastle, who preferred to keep up the nearby Clumber estate, and the house fell into decay.

Castle Farm:

Built half a mile to the south-east of the house, it was designed in 1758 by the Duchess of Norfolk.

Whitwell:

The village appeared in the Anglo Saxon Chronicles as *Hwitan Wylles Great* "the shining stream in the valley". The well across the square on the corner of Station Road reputedly had the sweetest water in the village. Prior to 1912 the water was carted in a horse-drawn tanker and sold for 1/2d a bucketful.

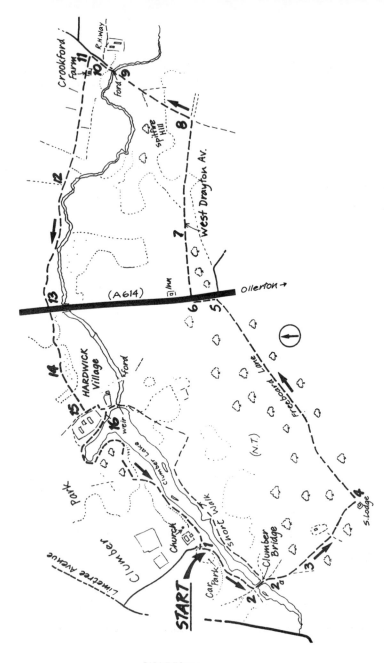

WALK 15

15. A Lake, a River and a Ford

A gentle ramble around Clumber Lake, alongside the River Poulter to picturesque Crookford.

THE FACTS

Area:	Clumber Park, River Poulter	
Distance:	Short Route:	6 km (3.75 miles)
	Long Route:	15km (9.25 miles)
Duration:	Short Route:	2 hours
	Long Route:	4.5 hours
Maps Required:	OS Pathfinder 763 (SK 67/77) Clumber Park & East Markham	
	OS Landranger 120 Mansfield and Worksop	
Bus/Train Link:	Worksop	
Terrain:	Mainly woodland paths and tracks, no steep hills	
Starting Point:	Main Car Park, Clumber Park SK 623744	
	(note: entrance charge to park your car, unless you are a National Trust Member) *This car park is scheduled to be moved in 1996 and it will be well signposted.*	
Refreshments:	Clumber House (National Trust), Clumber Park Hotel	

THE ROUTE

1.   Walk down from the car park to Clumber Lake, turn right and follow the lakeside path until you reach Clumber Bridge. Walk over Clumber Bridge.

2.   If you are following the **long route** cross over Clumber Bridge, cross the road

and take the road signposted to South Lodge. Continue along this road for 1.2 km to reach South Lodge.

2a. *If you are following the* **short route** turn immediately left and walk along the road at first to reach the car park, then go through a bar gate and continue along a clear path at the side of the lake until you reach woods, then the ford, over which you cross a bridge to reach Hardwick village (the short route joins the long route at this point, follow description from here at paragraph 8).

3.   Go through the fine metal gates of South Lodge to join the route of the Robin Hood Way. Turn left along a track: Freeboard Lane. Continue along this path for 2.4 km towards the A614. Just before the main road, turn left to follow a path and track left through the woods to come out at Drayton Gates (entrance to Clumber Park). Turn right and **carefully** cross the A614 main road to the path opposite, this is West Drayton Avenue.

4.   Follow the track, ignoring all others for 1.75 km, eventually in open countryside a farm track joins from the right. Turn left here at the bridleway sign and cross a field, following power cables and aiming for a gap in the plantation ahead.

5.   At the far side of the wood, bear slightly right to join a track on the right, heading downhill to a ford on the River Poulter. This is Crookford, an ideal place for a rest. Carry on uphill along a tarmac road to reach a bridleway on the left. Turn down the track passing Crookford Farm and keep on this well-defined track over open fields (the woods on the left are called Spitfire Bottoms). Continue ahead to join with and pass through another conifer plantation still keeping to a well-defined track.

6.   We continue along the track to eventually reach the bank of the River Poulter (a delightful spot). The track is easily followed towards the A614 and Clumber Park which can be seen ahead. On reaching the A614, cross the road **with care** to enter a wood. Go through a gate and follow a well-defined path through the wood keeping to the edge of the wood. On reaching the far end of the wood, go slightly left along the field edge path to reach a gap in the hedge onto a tarmacked road.

7.   Keep left and continue alongside the wood as the tarmac road leaves on the right. Continue in the same direction on a grass track across the fruit farm to reach a gate into Hardwick Grange (if you have time, have a look around the village). Turn left and walk 130 metres to reach a road leading to a car park (and to join the

Robin Hood Way). Turn right at this junction, and walk forward to reach Clumber Lake and toilets. *You also join the short walk at this point, coming in from the left across the weir.*

8.   Turn right, or straight on if on the short route, and follow the path around the lake along the wood edge on a well-established path, returning past Clumber Church and the site of Clumber House, beyond which lies the starting point and car park.

POINTS OF INTEREST

Clumber Estate formed part of Sherwood Forest until in 1707 licence was given to enclose it as a park for the queen's use. It was not developed until the mid 18th century. It is now owned by the National Trust. Clumber House was sited near a large, serpentine lake created in 1774-89. The park ornamentation includes a Greek Doric Temple, a three-arched stone bridge and cascade, a Roman Doric seat and a grotto. At the north-eastern end of the lake is the late 19th century estate village of *Hardwick in Clumber.*

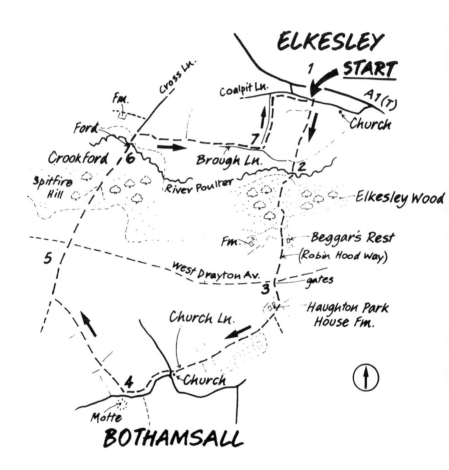

WALK 16

16. The Poulter Basin

An easy walk, chiefly on the sandstone of the Clumber Estate, taking in the modern village of Elkesley and the ancient settlement of Bothamsall. The picturesque situation of Crookford, a ford over the river Poulter, makes an ideal setting for a picnic.

THE FACTS

Area:	Elkesley, Bothamsall, Crookford
Distance:	8 km (5 miles)
Duration:	2.5 hours
Maps Required:	OS Pathfinder 763 (SK 67/77) Clumber Park & East Markham;
	OS Landranger 120 Mansfield & Worksop
Bus/Train Link:	Retford
Terrain:	Flat, easy walking on field paths and forest tracks
Starting Point:	Elkesley Village Hall Car Park SK 687756
Refreshments:	Robin Hood Inn, Elkesley

THE ROUTE

1. From the car park walk down the left-hand side of the recreation ground to emerge onto Brough Lane and turn right for 250 metres to a footpath sign on the left.

2. Follow the fence left downhill to a footbridge to enter Elkesley Wood. A well-defined path, indicated by blue way-mark posts, leads to the "Beggar's Rest", an old gamekeeper's cottage and up a cart track to West Drayton Avenue.

3. Pass through the gate opposite following the wide track which bears right in

front of Haughton Park House Farm. Ignore the entrance drive left and continue forward for 1 km on a green lane to enter the village of Bothamsall by the church.

4.   Proceed forward through the village and at the top of the hill, opposite the site of a motte and bailey castle, take the field path right as signed. This crosses an arable field for 350 metres to meet a hedge (aim for the middle transmission line pole.) Continue in the same direction, keeping the hedge on your left, to meet another track. Turn right and in 400 metres cross over West Drayton Avenue again.

5.   Cross over to follow the line of telegraph poles aiming for a gap in the trees ahead. Forward for 300 metres to the forest clearing, then bear right and left to join a good track which leads to the beautiful village of Crookford.

6.   Taking the bridge over the Poulter walk uphill for 150 metres and turn right up the metal road to the farm. Just in front of the gates take the narrow path, left, to emerge onto Brough Lane which you follow for 1 km to a fork at the edge of the village.

7.   Turn left up Lawnwood Lane then forward along Headland Avenue to a T-junction. Turn right along the road to join High Street and opposite the Pottery take the signed drive back to the village hall.

POINTS OF INTEREST

West Drayton Avenue was one of the favourite drives of the Newcastle Family when in their heyday at Clumber, stretching from the lakeside House to the mausoleum at Milton.

Bothamsall, a Newcastle estate village, was a one-time winner of the "Best kept village in Nottinghamshire" competition, as can be seen from the sign in the churchyard.

Bothamsall Church of St. Peter and St. Mary, rebuilt in 1845 on the site of an earlier church.

Elkesley: the Church of St. Giles.

17. Trent Valley Amble

An easy walk along the banks of the Trent linking the two villages of Dunham on Trent and Church Laneham.

THE FACTS

Area:	Dunham on Trent, Church Laneham
Distance:	8 km (5 miles)
Duration:	2.5 hours
Maps Required:	OS Pathfinder 764 (SK 87/97) Lincoln & Saxilby
	OS Landranger 121 Lincoln
Terrain:	A gentle walk along field paths
Starting Point:	Bridge Inn, Dunham on Trent SK 814745
	Park with care in the village
Refreshments:	Bridge Inn, White Swan Hall public house, Dunham on Trent; Ferryboat Inn, Church Laneham
Nearest Town:	Retford

THE ROUTE

1. Walk towards the toll-bridge passing St. Giles' Church. Take the footpath on the left before the toll-bridge and follow the floodbank path. You are walking along Dunham Rack. You follow a clear path for 2.6 km to the next village, Church Laneham.

2. On reaching Manor Farm, take the path to the right of the farm, past the orchard to reach a stile in the corner, going into the churchyard of St. Peters. Follow the path along the churchyard (hedge on right) to go over the stile, dropping down

57

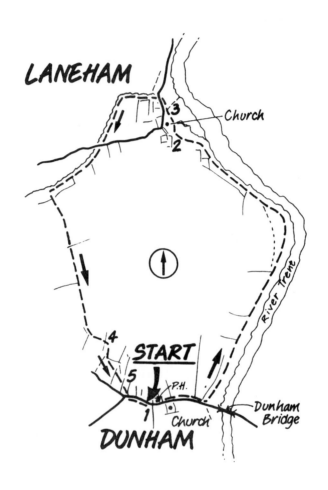

LANEHAM

Church

River Trent

START

P.H.

Dunham
Bridge

Church

DUNHAM

WALK 17

over the paddock and past a row of chalets to reach the road opposite the Ferryboat Inn. *(Note: the lane to the right drops down to the Trent and was the site of the ferry to cross the Trent into Lincolnshire.)*

3.   Walk past the churchyard and pub passing a small caravan site on one side and public toilets on the other. Follow the road to a sign on the left and follow the track along Laneham Beck to reach a road. Turn left and cross over the bridge, turning right to walk along the floodbank beside a stream. On reaching the stile turn left along the field edge crossing over a bridge and continue along another field edge path joining a farm track which turns towards Manor Farm, Dunham.

4.   The lane swings right as you reach the farm buildings, then go slightly left to cross a fence and follow an edge of a field. On reaching the gateway, aim in a straight line across a farm track then follow a hedge and go left at the corner (definitive line). It is easier to turn left at the track, go over the stile and footbridge.

5.   Go over two further fields, with the hedge on the left, then over an arable field to reach a twitchell. Turn right to leave a small estate, and then turn left along the path, then right to pass an old garden wall. On reaching the A17 you turn left to reach our starting point.

POINTS OF INTEREST

Dunham on Trent:

Dunham-on-Trent stands on the Nottinghamshire side of the River Trent, and on the opposite bank of the Trent is Lincolnshire, the two counties being linked by a toll bridge. The parish church of St. Oswald was built in the 15th century, although only the tower remains of the original building, as it has been rebuilt twice since.

Coronation Terrace at the foot of the bridge was built in 1911 to replace a row of thatched cottages. Their name commemorates the coronation of King George V and Queen Mary.

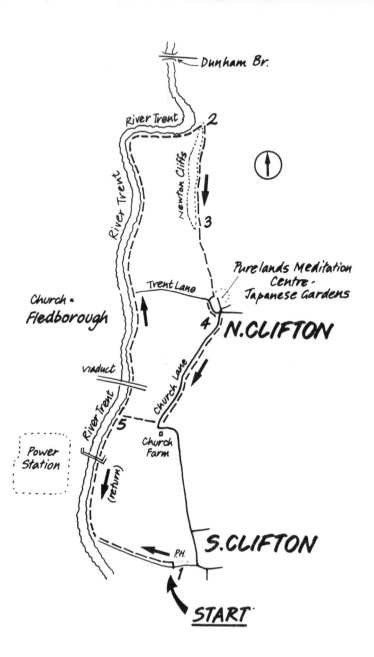

WALK 18

18. Newton Cliffs and the Japanese Garden

A superb Trentside walk taking in Newton cliffs, the unique Japanese garden and the classical, ornamental gates at the entrance to South Clifton Church.

THE FACTS

Area:	North and South Clifton
Distance:	10 km (6 miles)
Duration:	3 hours
Maps Required:	OS Pathfinder 764 (SK 87/97) Lincoln & Saxilby
	OS Landranger 121 Lincoln
Bus/Train Link:	Lincoln/Newark
Terrain:	Easy riverside and field paths
Starting Point:	The Red Lion, South Clifton SK 821702
Refreshments:	The Red Lion, South Clifton

THE ROUTE

1.   From the Red Lion walk westwards along Trent Lane to the river. Turn right and follow the floodbank to within 700 metres of Dunham Bridge.

2.   Turn right up the bank. Once on top, turn right again to head southwards over the red sandstone which forms Newton Cliffs. Continue ahead passing a triangulation point, right, then after 800 metres angle slightly right downhill to a stile.

3.   Over the stile head almost due south, pass to the right of a copse and cross a stile to enter a twitchell in North Clifton. Bear left to emerge onto the main street

adjacent to Purelands Meditation Centre with its unusual Japanese garden.

4.   Turn left to the green, and then follow Church Lane to South Clifton. At the church pass through the ornate iron gates to go to the footpath sign beyond the church. Cross the stile and head westwards, eventually going through a gate to attain the floodbank alongside the river.

5.   Turn left along the floodbank and retrace your steps to your starting point.

POINTS OF INTEREST

The highlight of the walk must be to include a visit to the unique **Purelands Meditation Centre Gardens**. Laid out in classical Japanese style with a miniature Mount Fuji at the entrance, the gardens give off an aura of peace and tranquility.

Newton Cliffs offer the walker tremendous views of the Trent Valley and on a clear day Lincoln Cathedral is clearly visible.

North and South Clifton:

The Church of St. George serves North and South Clifton and is entirely on its own between the two villages. Its tower dates from the 13th century in its lower stage, and the 15th century above. Eight tall pinnacles crown the tower. Inside, an oak reredos shows the Nativity, and a quaint old image bracket in the aisle is carved with flowers and a cat-like face with its tongue out.

19. Queen Eleanor Walk

A walk in the extreme north-east of Nottinghamshire, linking two isolated parishes, close to the cathedral city of Lincoln.

THE FACTS

Area: Harby and Thorney

Distance: 11 km (6.75 miles)

Duration: 3.5 hours

Maps Required: OS Pathfinder 764 (SK 87/97) Lincoln & Saxilby

                         Landranger 121 Lincoln

Bus/Train Link: Lincoln

Terrain: Flat

Starting Point: Glass & Bottle public house, Harby SK 880707

Refreshments: Glass & Bottle, Harby

THE ROUTE

1.   From the Glass & Bottle, turn right, then right again towards Saxilby. Cross the stile left and after the grass field aim half-right to a stile and footbridge and continue the same line. After the next stile and plank bridge, turn left to cross the Ox Pasture Drain by the farm bridge, then follow the line of stiles to continue diagonally through two fields. At this point, cross the route of an abandoned railway and cross one more field to the new bridge over a wide drain.

2.   Then follow the right-hand hedge, keeping to the right side, and continue almost straight ahead to Plot Farm, where there is an earth bridge over the dyke. Pass the farm and follow the farm track to the left. Turn left at the T-junction and on reaching the drive to Castle Farm on your right, turn right but aim to pass just left of the buildings. The path passes a pond and goes through Glover's

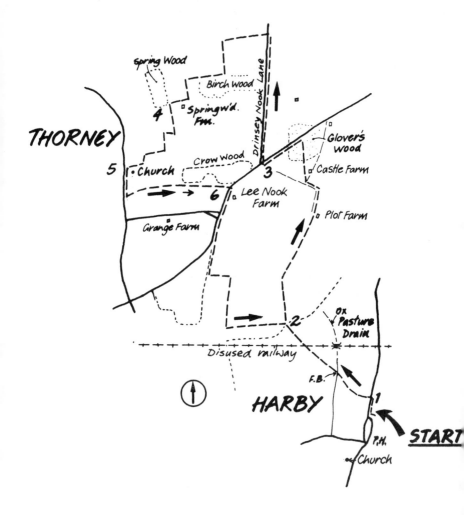

WALK 19

Wood to Sand Lane. Turn left to a road junction, then right.

3.   Walk up Drinsey Nook Lane as far as a signpost on the left, just before a chicken penitentiary. Here you follow one of the most jagged paths in the county. Pass a house and continue at the edge of an arable field. About two-thirds of the way along, a path at a bridge goes left across the field. Turn right at the other side and follow the edge of this field and the next. Left turn here on a grassy track, then right on a farm track past Springwood Farm to the corner of a wood.

4.   Cross the footbridge left and keep to the left of the hedge ahead, watching out for rabbit-holes. Turn right briefly at the end and left as way-marked, then look out for a stile on your right into a grass field. After following the wooded edge to another stile, you are guided by a fence to the end of a cul-de-sac and walk along it to Thorney.

5.   Turn left along the street, and shortly after St. Helen's Church go left again as signposted. A long path follows the edge of a grass field, passing a ha-ha with glimpses of lakes and gardens, then an arable field. A pleasant grassy track now leads to a lane, where you turn right past Lee Nook Farm.

6.   Go through a gateway just before a wood on your left, then follow the track along the wood, then left, then right. At the end of the track, follow the edge of the field left to the new bridge.

7.   Now retrace your route to Harby (see note below, and visit the local church).

POINTS OF INTEREST

A diversion, from the described route, should be made to visit the church in **Harby and All Saints Church** which was built around 1875. In the east wall of the tower there is a statue to *Eleanor of Castile* who died in 1290 at the house of Richard de Weston, which is the moated site to the east of the church. No trace of an Eleanor cross remains (they were erected at each site the bier stopped on her return to London). An information board, in front of the Church gives details of the Queen's funeral procession route.

The village also has a windmill from c1877.

Thorney: St. Helen's Church was built around 1849, with two 15th century arcades from the old church have been re-erected in the churchyard.

20. Nottinghamshire's Shrine of Our Lady

The walk circumnavigates Egmanton Wood with attractive deciduous trees and ancient hedges on its edge, and visits Moorhouse, a hamlet with a church in a field. An optional extension may be made to Laxton.

THE FACTS

Area:	Egmanton, Laxton, Moorhouse
Distance:	7.4 km (4.2 miles) Additional 3.5km (2 miles) with extension to Laxton
Duration:	2 hours (3 hours with extension)
Maps Required:	OS Pathfinder (SK 66/76) Ollerton
	OS Landranger 120 Mansfield & Worksop
Bus/Train Link:	Mansfield
Terrain:	Easy, but muddy if weather has been wet
Starting Point:	Egmanton Church SK 736689 It may be possible to park at the Parish Hall situated 100 metres past the Church, turn right by the last lamp-post in the village. Please check on arrival.
Refreshments:	None (At the time of writing, the public house in Egmanton is closed. However, there is a public house in Laxton, The Dovecote Inn.)

THE ROUTE

1.   Take the footpath across the road opposite the gate of the Church. Cross the field, aiming for the footpath sign visible. At the end of the field cross a footbridge and road, entering the lane (Wood Lane) going due south towards Egmanton

wood. When it turns right, you bear left into a field, crossing diagonally, making for the north-east corner of the wood.

2.   Pass through a gateway and keep round the wood edge until you reach the south-east corner.

3.   Here, a footbridge to the right crosses the watercourse and takes a path on the southern edge of the wood, but we turn left and continue on the field boundary following the stream, crossing a footbridge and stile until we come to a stile on the right by an oak tree. Go over the stile and cross the field diagonally to the left hand corner, to a stile, footbridge and stile again near a high-voltage pylon. Turn right and follow the hedge, passing through the first hedged field boundary, until you reach a second straggly hedge. Pass through and turn left along it. Take the stile onto the road, turn right then shortly on the left there is a gate to the Church in a field.

4.   Retrace your steps across the field, through the gate, turn left then right on a minor road to Laxton for approximately 1 km. At a left hand bend in the road, a footpath sign on the right leads into a field by a track to East Park Wood. (Don't follow the track.) Turn left along the footpath following the field boundary on your left until you reach a grassy track.

5.   Turn left along the field boundary, passing two hedges on your right, then halfway along the next hedge pass through the gate turning right. Cross the field and leave it at the top left-hand corner through the gap in the hedge. You will see the track ahead a few metres to your left between two fields. Continue straight ahead to reach the track around the west edge of Egmanton Wood. You will soon enter the lane which bends round to meet the point where you left it at paragraph 2 above.

6.   Retrace your steps to Egmanton Church.

Optional extension into Laxton

At paragraph 5, continue west instead of turning through the gate and you will reach Laxton main street in about 1 km, turn right for public house, etc.

POINTS OF INTEREST

Egmanton:

The 14th century church of St. Mary set amongst great chestnut trees in the middle of the village, was given a sumptuous restoration in 1896 by the young Ninian (later Sir) Comper, under the patronage of the high-church Duke of Newcastle. They restored the shrine which had been constructed to commemorate a vision of the Blessed Virgin - seen in the wood, which was then renamed Ladywood - until it was destroyed during the reign of Henry VIII. Ladywood still exists but unfortunately cannot be visited as rights of way to it do not pass. Enjoy the rood, organ-case, pulpit and stained glass (some modern and some ancient). *Details of where to obtain the key to visit the Church are displayed on the door.*

Nearby is *Gaddick Hill*, a well-preserved motte and bailey.

Moorhouse:

The present Church in the Field was built in 1861 and is a daughter to the Church of St. Michael at Laxton. *The key to the Church may be obtained by asking at the farm.*

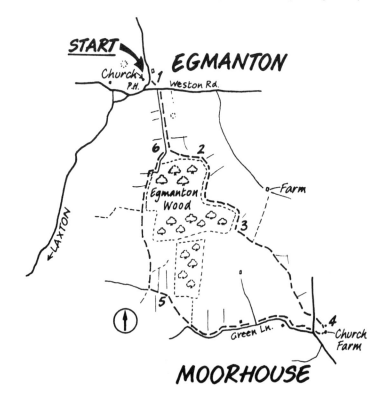

WALK 20

21. The Medieval Open Fields of Laxton

A ramble around the unique three field system of farming, as carried out at Laxton since Medieval times.

THE FACTS

Area:	Laxton
Distance:	12 km (7.5 miles)
Duration:	3.75 hours
Maps Required:	OS Pathfinder 780 (SK 66/76) Ollerton)
	OS Landranger 120 Mansfield & Worksop
Bus/Train Link:	Mansfield
Terrain:	Footpaths over cornfields, meadows and green lanes. No steep climbs.
Starting Point:	Visitors Centre Car Park, adjacent to the Dovecote Inn. SK 724671
Refreshments:	Dovecote Inn, Laxton

THE ROUTE

1.   Turn left from the Visitors' Centre and call in the Pinfold, next to the Dovecote Inn. Walk 50 metres further, climb a stile on your left and walk up a path at right angles to the road. Climb two more stiles, keeping the hedge on your right. Climb a stile set in the hedge on your right, and continue in the same direction, but on the other side of the hedge.

2.   Turn right at the top, by the cricket pavilion and walk in a straight line through the gate, then climb four stiles. After the fourth stile, turn left and keeping

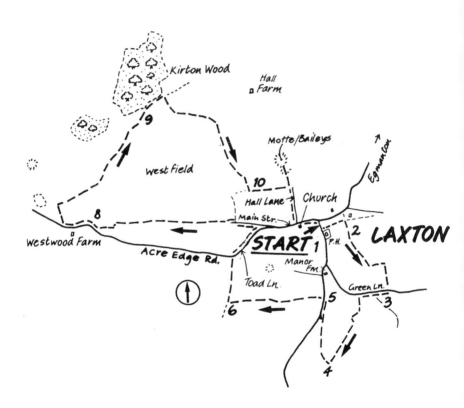

WALK 21

the hedge on your left, walk another 100 metres and go through a gap in the hedge in front of you. After walking another 100 metres on the same line, turn right and walk down a cart track to the road.

3.   Turn right at the road and walk 300 metres to a footpath sign and stile on your left. Climb this, walk over the meadow to a footbridge over a stream, then veer right to walk down a cart track, keeping to the left of the hedge.

4.   At the end climb the stile on your right and walk down a small meadow to cross a bridge into a large field. Walk over this field, making for the gate to the road which is in the far left-hand hedge. Turn right at the road and walk 150 metres.

5.   Turn left and walk up the green lane for 400 metres. You are now in the Mill Field *see note in Points of Interest).* Walk along the track on the same line for 500 metres to a junction. *Pause at this and look in front of you at the top of the rise and observe a small clump of conifer trees. This is the site of the mill from which Mill Field takes its name.*

6.   Turn right down this stone track and walk across to the Laxton/Ollerton Road.

7.   Turn right down the road and then turn left in 400 metres at the next junction. Walk along the lane to join a track on the extreme left-hand edge of a large expanse of land. Walk along this track for 1 km then turn left as the hedge goes left, and in 50 metres turn right and then walk across the field towards the cottage by the road side.

8.   Turn right down the road for 250 metres, then right again keeping the hedgerow on your right. After 200 metres go through on the right, and walk across two fields as way-marked. After the second field, walk along the grassy sike which runs along the edge of the West Field to a stile into a meadow with the edge of Kirton Wood in front of you.

9.   Cross this and the next one, keeping Kirton Wood on your left and when halfway across the third meadow opposite the footbridge, turn to your right and head for the top left-hand corner of a narrow meadow. Climb the stile and walk over the hill, aiming for the far right-hand corner of a large field. At this point, go through the gateway and turn half-right to walk along the left-hand hedge of a small field. At the end, go across the long, narrow field in front of you, aiming for the top left-hand corner. After climbing the stile, cross the footbridge and then

cross the field diagonally on the same line to the hedge corner. Walk up the rest of the field on the same line to a stile in the hedge on your left. Climb the stile into a grass meadow, turn right and pass through a wooden gate.

10. Turn left and climb the fence at the side of the large gate into a green lane. Follow this along until it swings right. Here you go through a gate on your left and walk down for 200 metres to the group of trees where you find one of the best examples of motte and bailey in the county, the Castle of the Everinghams. Retrace your steps to where the green lane turns right and leads you to St. Michael's Church. On leaving, turn left where a path from the churchyard leads you back to the Visitors' Centre and Car Park.

POINTS OF INTEREST

Laxton:

The area is well-known for retaining the three-field system of crop rotation whereby the large fields, known as the West Field, Mill Field and the South Field are divided into narrow strips. Much of the land hereabouts is still owned by the Crown and an impressive Visitor Centre behind the Dovecote Inn gives a full description of this unique farming system.

Mill Field: is the oldest and the largest of the Three Great Fields. This was laid down in 1189 and consists of 196 acres divided into 68 strips. The mill which gave the field its name blew down in 1913, the last miller being Mr. James Laughton. When the field is designated as the Fallow Field for that year, seeds are undersown with corn, which is allowed under the modern system, but they must be cut and harvested by 1st July in order to allow the land to have its customary rest.

The **Pinfold** was traditionally where animals were placed when lost, and now contains a plan of the village lands.

St. Michael's Church is well worth a visit. Inside are monuments to the de Everingham family. On the tomb of Adam, who died in 1341, his first wife's effigy is in stone, like his own, but that of his second wife is in oak, which is the only Medieval wooden effigy in the county.

Castle of the Everinghams Earthworks of a motte and bailey caste. This castle site offers a fine view of Lincoln Cathedral.

22. In Robin Hood's Footsteps

A walk through fields and forest including two of the old great estates of the Dukeries, namely Thoresby, the seat of the Manvers family and Rufford, the seat of the Savile family. It also calls at two Visitors' Centres.

THE FACTS

Area:	Rufford Park, Edwinstowe
Distance:	13.5 km (8.5 miles)
Duration:	4.25 hours
Maps Required:	OS Pathfinder 780 (SK 66/76) Ollerton
	OS Landranger 120 Mansfield & Worksop
Bus/Train Link:	Mansfield
Terrain:	Forest bridleways and field footpaths, no climbing
Starting Point:	Rufford Mill car park SK 647656 **Note:** there is a charge in summer
Refreshments:	Sherwood Visitors' Centre; Rufford Visitors' Centre; Robin Hood Inn, Edwinstowe

THE ROUTE

1.   From Rufford Mill car park go up to the lake, turn left and follow the lakeside path, over the bridge and turn left to the road, and go down the signed bridleway on your left in a northerly direction. Walk along this well-defined path until you reach the main A614 road. **Carefully** cross the road at the railway bridge.

2.   Walk alongside the railway on its southern side and after 1 km at the signal-box, when you are opposite Thoresby Colliery, cross the railway **with care** at the level crossing and follow the farm track which passes a farm and a group of cottages, to the main Ollerton-Edwinstowe road near the entrance to Thoresby Colliery.

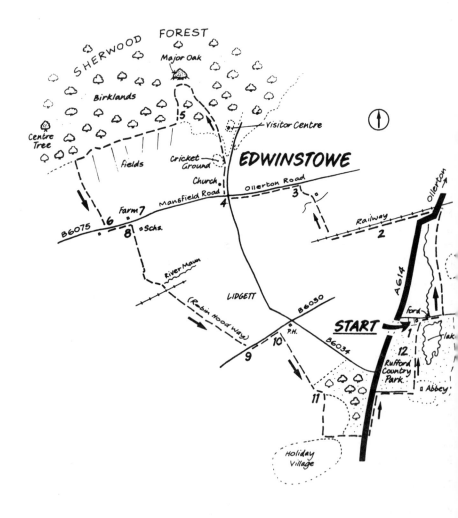

SHERWOOD FOREST

Major Oak

Birklands

Centre Tree

fields

5

Visitor Centre

Cricket Ground

EDWINSTOWE

Church

Ollerton Road

3

Mansfield Road

4

B6075

Farm 7

6

8 □ Schs.

Railway

2

Ollerton

A614

River Maun

(Robin Hood Way)

LIDGETT

B6030

ford

9

10

P.H.

B6034

START

1

lak

12

Rufford Country Park

11

□ Abbey

Holiday Village

WALK 22

3.   Turn left and walk along the road which leads you into Edwinstowe.

4.   Turn right at the traffic lights into Church Street, cross the road at the entrance to the Sherwood Forest Country Park. Take the way-marked path to the Visitors' Centre clearly marked on your left. Follow the signed route to the Major Oak, then turn right due south on a path way-marked Edwinstowe for 300 metres to the end of the trees.

5.   Turn right onto a bridleway, then immediately take the left fork onto a way-marked track on the edge of the Forest running in a westerly direction. Continue on this track for 1 km until you come to a path junction with a well-marked path leading to the left.

6.   Go down this field edge path leading to the A6075, where you turn left.

7.   Walk along for 250 metres until you come to Villa Real Farm on your left.

8.   Cross the road at the farm gate and go down a signed green lane opposite. Follow the lane to the right and turn left to cross two bridges which span the River Maun. You are now on the Robin Hood Way. After 200 metres where the path divides, take the right-hand fork which will lead you over the railway level crossing and down onto a road. Cross this and rejoin the path on the other side, passing Holly Farm, and continue until you reach a road - the B6030.

9.   Turn left and walk for 400 metres until you reach the entrance to South Forest on your left. The Robin Hood public house is on the corner by the traffic lights.

10. Turn right and walk down a signposted path. Continue on this through the corner of Broad Oak Break, bear left and then right following a field boundary in a southerly direction until you come to a green lane.

11. Turn left on this and after 100 metres you join the entrance road to the Centre Parc Holiday Complex. Carry on for 50 metres and where this drive veers to the left, walk round the side of the large metal gates onto a road marked "Private". After walking 150 metres you come to the main A614 road. Cross this road with **extreme care** and turn left along the roadside path to the main entrance of Rufford Park, which you enter along the main driveway to the Abbey and stable block.

12. To complete the walk there are two options:

a.   Walk through the Craft Centre to visit Hugh Greenway Garden and join the linking path to Rufford Lake, and so back to Rufford Mill and the car park.

b.   Turn left before the Abbey, go through an L-shaped pergola, over a moat and continue along the broad ride and return to the Mill.

POINTS OF INTEREST

Edwinstowe:

The village is in the heart of Sherwood Forest, which following the Norman Conquest became the Royal Hunting Forest, covering about a fifth of Nottinghamshire. The law forbade hunting and felling of trees, and a special court set up the village to deal with minor offenses tried 119 men in 1334 for venison trespass and many for taking oak trees. The village is famous for its connections with Robin Hood. He was reputed to have married Maid Marion at the Church of St. Mary, Edwinstowe.

Rufford Abbey was occupied for 400 years by the Cistercian monks and since then for a further 400 years by the Savile family. Interesting things to see include ice houses, animal graves and a flock of Mouflon sheep.

Thoresby Colliery was sunk in 1925 and is one of the remaining viable collieries in the county.

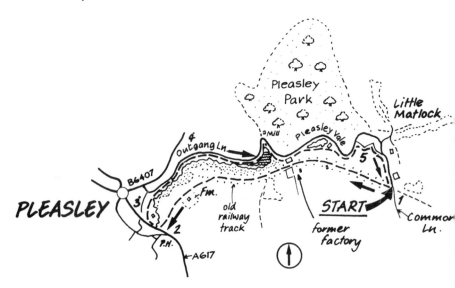

WALK 23

23. The Mills of Pleasley Vale

Just outside Mansfield, the Vale offers a haven of quiet to retired miners and visitors alike. The Viyella factories, left in a state of decay after a take-over, hope for better things, while paths beside the river Meden and along a disused railway are well worth a detour.

THE FACTS

Area:	Pleasley
Distance:	6 km (3.5 miles)
Duration:	1.5 hours
Maps Required:	OS Pathfinder 779 (SK 46/56) Mansfield North
	OS Landranger 120 Mansfield & Worksop
Bus/Train Link:	Mansfield
Terrain:	Very easy walking
Starting Point:	Car Park on Common Lane, Mansfield (approach via Vale Road) SK 527646
Refreshments:	The Olde Plough, Pleasley

THE ROUTE

1.   The first part of the walk is north-west through the car park along the Meden Trail, with glimpses of past industry below, including a very tall chimney with a cone top. Continue along the trail, ignoring two paths leading off. Just after the pylon on the right, and before the trail crosses a bridge, turn left over a stile and ascend diagonally right up a field, which may contain horses, leading to a stone stile beside a farm gate and Wren Hill Farm. The views from this point, over Pleasley and its vale, are worth the effort.

2.   Pass the duck pond at the farm, cross another stone stile and follow the access road down to the A617. *At this point, The Olde Plough public house can be seen across the road to the left, while just to the right is a tunnel to take you safely under the road to the Inn.* The walk continues past the tunnel and to the right along the Vale beside the River Meden.

3.   Go past the first bridge, cross the second and third bridges and up the steps to the top path.

4.   Continue along the woodland path. Turn left over a fourth bridge and mill stream, then turn right along the woodland path until it joins Outgang Lane. Turn right to follow the lane past the sad remains of stone houses and the white hulk of the owner's house, then the works which now await new industry. Beyond these is the War Memorial, where you turn right past the Old Post Office, along a path between a stone wall and a cliff, and then past an attractive row of Victorian cottages.

5.   Just beyond the cottages rejoin the road. Your starting point is just around the corner to the right.

POINTS OF INTEREST

Pleasley Vale is an important site of industrial archaeology. The original mill was built in 1765 by three Nottingham businessmen and Mansfield drapers. Although a lower mill was added in 1798, sadly both were burnt down in the 1840s. They were replaced by the buildings that can be seen today and were part of the International Viyella Group, together with examples of mid 19th century company housing and amenities.

24. Bess of Hardwick / Lady Chatterley's Walk

A circular walk linking the Pleasley Trails network with the beautiful Park of Hardwick Hall in all its splendour, and the longer walk linking the manorial village of Teversal with its fine manor once belonging to the Molyneux and Carnaervon families and the fictional home of D.H. Lawrence's Lady Chatterley.

THE FACTS

Area:	Rowthorne, Ault Hucknall, Hardwick Park	
	Long Walk: also Teversal	
Distance:	Long Walk	15.2 km (9.5 miles)
	Short Walk	12 km (7.5 miles)
Duration:	Long Walk	5 hours
	Short Walk	4 hours
Maps Required:	OS Pathfinder 779 (SK 46/47) Mansfield (North) & Part of Sherwood Forest	
	OS Landranger 120 Mansfield & Worksop	
Bus/Train Link:	Mansfield	
Terrain:	Field paths, parklands and railway tracks. Some moderate climbing.	
Starting Point:	Rowthorne Trail Car Park SK 476647	
Refreshments:	Hardwick Inn, Hardwick Hall; Carnaervon Arms, Teversal	

THE ROUTE

1.   From the car park take the path past the Trail notice board and enter the Trail proper. Turn right after going through a kissing gate and walk along the Trail to reach a stile and junction of paths. Turn left and enter an open field, and walk uphill in a slightly left diagonal direction. On reaching the top of the hill turn around to see your first view of Hardwick Hall in all its glory! Our route now crosses the field to a stile seen straight ahead in a midpoint between two pylons. Cross two further fields in the same direction to reach the road (Field Lane).

2.   Turn left and walk along Field Lane to enter Rowthorne village. At the junction turn right and pass through part of the village with lovely houses and take the footpath on the left at the side of Haven Hill House. Go through a field gate, over a stile and straight on across the field aiming for its right-hand corner. Over the stile and stream and follow the field edge path, with the hedge on the right, to reach the road (Dukes Drive).

3.   Cross the road and take the footpath opposite going over two fields with stiles to reach the road at the edge of the village of Ault Hucknall (look over the hedge to see Bolsover Castle in the distance). Turn left and walk into the village, going past St. John the Baptist Church to reach a bridleway on the right side of the graveyard.

4.   Walk down the bridleway to reach a house (The Grange) and just after a gate, walk into a field, turn left and walk across the field following the fence and in the direction of Hardwick Hall. On reaching a stile on the left just before a cattle grid and road, take this and turn right going over the road and continuing down to a kissing gate on the right.

5.   Go through the gate and take the footpath downhill to arrive at a series of fishponds *(note at the end of the second fishpond, notice the ice-house on the bank)*. Continue downhill to a gate to meet a bridleway coming in on the right and continue straight on to a path junction *(note the quarry on the right, used to build the new Hardwick Hall)*.

6.   At the junction turn right and walk along the trails around Miller's Pond. At the far end of the lake turn left and walk across a dam, then left going over stepping stones into the car park. Continue straight on to reach the Information Centre and toilets.

7.   Turn left and go through a barrier gate to arrive at the junction previously

visited. Turn right this time then right again before a gate to go along another dam to a lake. *This lake is known as "Great Pond".* At the far end of the dam look up towards the two Hardwick Halls *(the best view for a photograph).* Take the path on the left to walk on a path at the side of the lake. Follow this along scrubland going into a wood and take the path over planks, previously a muddy area. At the bend in the track look at the next pond - Decoy Pond. *(Note the building with the steps down to confine the nets and ropes.)* Turn left and walk out of the woods through the kissing gate, then turn right, following the boundary of the wood through parkland to the Hardwick Inn. After your refreshments, return to the cattle grid and cross parkland aiming for stone steps seen ahead on the slope. If you do not visit the Hardwick Inn, when leaving the wood from Decoy Pond, go straight on uphill to the steps seen ahead.

8.   Walk up the steps then continue to climb uphill on an obvious path line to arrive at a kissing gate. Through this, and straight uphill to arrive at a large, green open space with the two Hardwick Halls in the foreground. Take an opportunity to view. Our route walks to the driveway, then turns right going between the two Halls, past the stables to drop downhill over a cattle grid past the workshops on the left to reach a corner of the driveway.

9.   Go through a gate on the left, enter a field and walk straight across with the path around the curve of land to arrive at a gate and stile. Over the stile and walk uphill into Lady Spencer's Wood. At the top of the rise, follow the path to the left and follow a clear path through the plantation (you are now in Nottinghamshire). At the far end of the plantation you climb uphill to reach a gate. Turn left along a track past Hardwick Park Farm to reach Norwood Lodge.

9a.   **Short Route:** *Over the stile and along the drive to the left of Norwood Lodge. Enter the field by a gate and walk straight across the field aiming for woodland seen ahead. Enter the wood and follow a clear path to reach a footbridge over a stream and to a stile. Over the stile and cross the field diagonally left to reach a further stile. Over this to join Rowthorne Trail. Walk to the stile on the left and walk down the Trail to return to the car park.*

10.   **Long Route:** Continue down the road to reach a footpath on the right. Cross a large field to reach the far field edge. Turn left and follow the field edge path (hedge on right) to the end of the field. Go through a gap seen ahead to enter a green lane, going over a former railway and to reach New Bound Lane.

11.   Turn right and walk 350 metres to a stile at the bottom of the hill. Over the stile

and across two fields to reach St. Catherine's Church. Cross the road and walk into the churchyard, which is well worth a visit. Continue out of the churchyard at the far side of the church, turn right and walk past Teversal Manor. Go through the gate seen ahead and along Buttery Lane to a road junction. Turn left and walk down to the railway bridge. **Do not** go under the bridge, but take the steps onto the railway. (Note the signs for Teversal Visitors' Centre.)

12. Turn right and walk along the Teversal Trail and follow the track to reach Newbound Lane. Go up a slope, turn right then left down a further slope, to continue along a track going through a cutting (Permian Lower Magnesian Limestone) and open out. Notice another railway on the left: this is the Rowthorne Trail. We arrive at a convenient track on the left, after which you join the Rowthorne Trail. Take this going over two stiles. Turn left and walk back along the delightful Rowthorne Trail (a last glimpse of Hardwick Hall is possible), crossing some stiles to arrive back at the car park.

POINTS OF INTEREST

Hardwick Halls, fishponds and ice-house:

Hardwick Hall was begun in 1591 by Elizabeth, Countess of Shrewsbury (Bess of Hardwick). The work was quickly completed, as the house was ready for occupation in 1597. Parapets incorporating her initials E.S. stand out against the sky. Bess was a much-married lady, gaining her first husband at the age of 12, and enriching herself with each match. Her fourth and last husband was George, Earl of Shrewsbury, who was for many years the custodian of the imprisoned Mary, Queen of Scots.

Bolsover Castle:

A castle has stood here since the reign of William the Conqueror, but nothing of the Norman building remains. The present Castle was begun during the reign of James I, with later additions.

Ault Hucknall: The church of St. John the Baptist dates from Saxon times, although it was not mentioned in the Domesday book. The west end of the church has several pieces of reused masonry, including a fine Saxon window.

Teversal:

This is a manorial village, belonging to the Molyneux and Carnaervon families.

The church of St. Catherine has a rare set of 17th century hatchments: panels bearing coats of arms, and the beautifully decorated Carnaervon Pew. There is also an underground crypt containing 12 leaded coffins of members of the Molyneux family dating from the 17th century. However, the crypt is rarely open to the public. There is the story of its patron saint in pictures carved around the doorway. In the graveyard, to the left of the porch, are 17th century gravestones.

Teversal was also the fictional home of D.H. Lawrence's Lady Chatterley, who supposedly met her gamekeeper lover in the woods around Hardwick Hall.

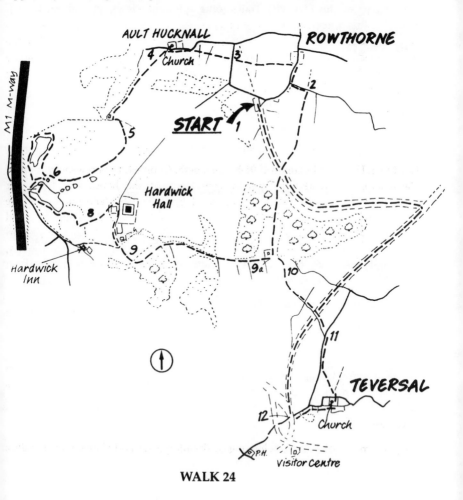

WALK 24

25. The Summit of Nottinghamshire

On the Nottinghamshire-Derbyshire border, this little walk takes you to the highest point in Nottinghamshire (205 metres!) near Tibshelf Wharf and follows a tiny part of the Five Pits Trail. Some splendid views, pity about the M1 invading this quiet corner.

THE FACTS

Area:	Tibshelf
Distance:	10 km (6 miles)
Duration:	3.5 hours
Maps Required:	OS Pathfinder 795 (SK 45/55) Sutton in Ashfield and 779 (SK 46/56) Mansfield North
	OS Landranger 120 Mansfield & Worksop
Bus/Train Link:	Sutton in Ashfield
Terrain:	Lots of hills and hollows, a lot of grass fields but some arable
Starting Point:	B6026 west of Huthwaite, near the entrance to Spring Farm SK 457591
Refreshments:	Four public houses in Tibshelf

THE ROUTE

1.   Cross the stile to the left of the farm drive, go ahead to a stile then diagonally across pasture. Go up the edges of two fields, turn right along a headland and round the corner. Cross an insignificant stile with a stone step and turn up hill, then along the top of the field to a stile. Cross the bridge over the M1 and look out for a stile on your right: cross two paddocks to reach Littlemoor Lane.

2.   Turn right after 25 metres turn left to a farm gate and across a grass field, the

left again beside a railway culvert. When the path swings right to cross the railway, walk past some woodland and veer left to a signboard for the Five Pits Trail. Don't turn here, but go on to two fishing ponds. *This is a good spot for a picnic, and if you go through the handgate ahead, and through the car park on the right, there is a picnic table.*

If you have to buy refreshments, pass the table and join the path on your left which leads to Tibshelf. A stile on the left brings you to the Wheatsheaf or the Royal Oak.

3. After this detour, return to the Trail and continue north to the edge of the village. Here a hedged path leads away right, just past the school playing-field. At a junction, turn left and follow the enclosed path to the end. Go ahead across a muddy field. Cross the stile and bridge and angle right to a stile, then head straight across the pasture. Another stile and turn right, then keep near the right-hand hedge in two fields before passing a stone barn to reach the Chesterfield Road.

4. Turn right for 150 metres crossing the road to a signpost near a bend. Go forward past the garden of number 58, admire the distant view of Hardwick Hall to the left, but cross the field half-right, continuing diagonally in the next field. Turn right here to pass between some houses and a strip of woodland, then left to recross the M1. After 100 metres climb the stile on the left and cross the arable field to another stile. Continue beside a hedge, then cross-field to a waymark in the hedge opposite.

5. Turn sharp right here and follow the field edge in this field and the next, crossing a stile into a small copse. Continue down Wharf Lane to the road, straight across, along a hedged path and along the left-hand edge of two fields. Near the top of the hill which is the summit of Nottinghamshire, swap sides of the hedge and go past a wood and reservoir. Half-way past this, angle left to a stile. Follow the road left, then turn right at the T-junction. After 200 metres take the stile on the right, cross the top of the grass field and angle left down the next.

6. Cross an arable field, aiming about 50 metres right of the corner, then follow the same line in the next field to a crossing over a disused railway line. After crossing, head half-left across two grass fields, but don't cross the next stile ahead. Turn right and keep to the high ground beside the deep valley, and watch out for a stile on the left near the foot of the next field. Your route is now up the hill to a gate, forward to another gate and then a stile, and down the hill to the road and your starting point.

POINTS OF INTEREST

The views along this walk are the main features: enjoy new vistas of Nottingham-shire and Derbyshire, including glimpses of Hardwick Hall.

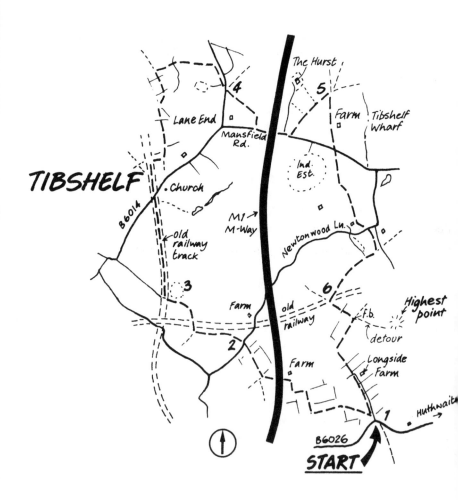

WALK 25

26. Nottinghamshire Dumbles

A circular walk in the highest part of the County offering distant views and visiting Portland Park, Castle Hill and Kirkby Dumble.

THE FACTS

Area:	Portland Park, Kirkby in Ashfield, Kirkby Dumbles
Distance:	11 km (7 miles)
Duration:	3.5 hours
Maps Required:	OS Pathfinder 795 (SK 45/55) Sutton in Ashfield
	OS Landranger 120 Mansfield & Worksop
Bus/Train Link:	Mansfield
Terrain:	Undulating field paths, some muddy tracks in winter
Starting Point:	Portland Park Visitors' Centre Car Park SK 501548 (access off Lindley's Lane, Kirkby in Ashfield opposite Ashfield District Council offices.
Refreshments:	Various public houses in Kirkby in Ashfield, and Portland Park Visitor Centre

THE ROUTE

1. From the car park follow the tarmac path signposted to the Portland Park Visitors' Centre Cafe (toilets and visitors features are available). Go through the gate ahead and take the upper path on the left (red route). Follow the path on high level with excellent views of Portland Park and its trees. Turn right at the junction and drop down to a tarmac path. Turn left and go over the stile and railway to cross a further stile into a field.

2. Go straight across two fields to reach a stile. Over this and climb up steep

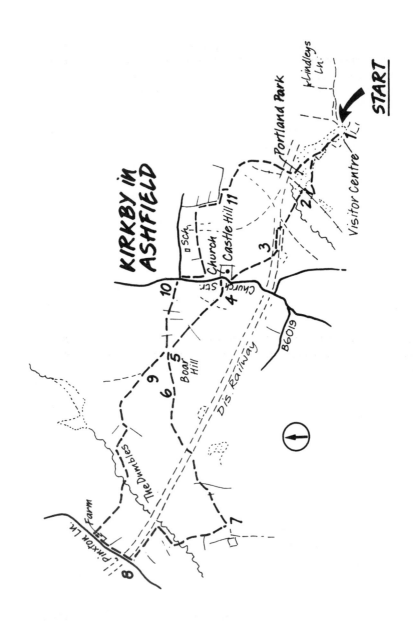

WALK 26

steps to a disused railway line (we describe here the legal line, but it is possible to *turn right then at the corner turn left to walk up the disused line to reach the junction*). Over the railway, drop down the other side into a gulley, turn left and out of scrubland into a field, follow the field edge path embankment on the right to the far edge of the field. Over the stile to join the previous route described.

3.   Take the path signposted uphill firstly following the hedge on the left, then turning right to cross a field and head for St. Wilfred's Church seen ahead. Go through the churchyard to the road (Church Street). Walk ahead to the Duke of Wellington public house.

4.   Cross the road and take the path to the right of St. Wilfred's Parish Hall. Follow this past a cul de sac to reach a wide track, from where you can enjoy distant views of Derbyshire. Turn right and follow the field edge path (hedge on right) to the end of the field, then left to reach a gap in the hedge. Turn right through a large gap and go diagonally across the field and walk well into the field to arrive at a track coming from the right.

5.   Turn left and walk up to the summit of Boar Hill. Drop down to reach a stile. Over the stile, walk diagonally across the field to the right-hand corner. Over the stile and take the path diagonally left to a stile at the other side of the field. Turn left and aim for the bridlegate. Through the gate and over a disused railway line to a further gate.

6.   Enter the next field and turn right, crossing this aiming for the right of the pylon seen on the skyline. On reaching the top of the field, go over a stile to then aim for the middle of the two visible pylons. You are aiming for the left-hand corner of the field to reach a stile and field gate.

7.   Turn right into the bridleway, then left through a bridlegate to drop down to a green lane into Kirkby Dumbles, to reach a bridle-bridge across a stream and walk 40 metres to take the footpath to the right. You now follow the field edge path with the Dumble and stream to the right. On reaching the embankment ahead, turn left to follow this for a few metres, then go straight across a field and head for the stile and road seen ahead (Crow Trees Farm is seen on the right).

8.   Turn right along Pinxton Lane and walk 220 metres to Crow Trees Farm. Turn right and walk through the farmyard and outbuildings and follow the field edge path (hedge on left) which you eventually leave to drop down into the Kirkby Dumble once again. Follow the green lane path out of the Dumble and climb uphill

firstly walking parallel to the stream then climbing steeply on eventually meeting the farm track entrance to The Dumbles bungalow. Continue straight on uphill to meet a footpath crossing the lane on the left. At this point look for the way-mark on the right and a gap in the hedge and enter the field.

9.   Our path crosses a large field heading in the direction of St. Wilfred's Church spire seen ahead. You join a path halfway across the field (previously walked). Turn left and continue in a straight line going into a green lane (Cow Pasture Lane) and continue to the road, keeping the hedge on your right.

10.   Turn right along Church Street passing the village cross and the entrance to Tichfield Park to reach Orchard Walk on the left-hand side of the road. Follow the footpath into Orchard Road. Turn right at the footpath (next to no. 7 Orchard Road). Drop down to the industrial estate access road. Turn right and then left up steps to reach Beech Avenue. Straight onto crossroads. Turn right along Wheatley Avenue and turn down Cedar Avenue, which is the second on the left. Turn down Birch Tree Crescent and take the footpath next to no. 1 Birch Tree Crescent.

11.   Take the footpath going over the stile into a field then going diagonally left towards the railway bridge. (At the time of writing, the Robin Hood Line was under construction, so the next section was not established.) Go over the railway bridge and turn right. You are now walking between two railway lines (Robin Hood Line is on the left). On reaching the junction of two paths, take the path uphill (way-marked) and on reaching the top of the hill and an open field, walk towards the pylon seen ahead. Turn left past the pylon and then right after 50 metres to drop downhill through an overgrown quarry to enter Portland Park. Take the second left (red way-marked post) and follow the path back to the Visitor Centre. Turn left along the tarmac road back to the car park.

POINTS OF INTEREST

Kirkby in Ashfield:

Little remains of the original village centre features. The Manor House of 1622 which stood opposite the church was demolished in 1964. The church of St. Wilfred was mostly destroyed by fire in 1907, with a little Medieval masonry surviving. Opposite the church is a stone pinfold, where stray animals were kept. The remains of the 13th century Stoteville Castle are to be found at Castle Hill Camp, immediately to the south of the church.

27. The Friar Tuck Trail

A pleasant woodland walk taking in the sites connected to the legendary Friar Tuck, one of Robin Hood's Merrie Men.

THE FACTS

Area:	Thieves Wood, Lindhurst
Distance:	7.2 km (4.5 miles)
Duration:	2.5 hours
Maps Required:	OS Pathfinder 795 (SK 45/55) Sutton in Ashfield;
	OS Landranger 120 Mansfield, Worksop
Bus/Train Link:	Mansfield
Terrain:	Forest tracks and fields
Starting Point:	Park on the grass verge in Ricket Lane, near the Robin Hood Scout Centre SK 565561
Refreshments:	Craft Centre, Portland Training Centre

THE ROUTE

1.   From the start of the walk return to take the footpath on the corner. Drop downhill along the field edge path to walk into Harlow Wood.

2.   After about 100 metres into the wood, there is a junction of paths, turn 90 right and follow that path for a further 100 metres to the next junction of paths. Here bear slightly to the right and continue along a path which stays just inside the wood. Along here, on the right amongst the rhododendron bushes there is the remains of a moat which surrounded the legendary home of Friar Tuck. Beyond the moat is the dried-out bed of what was once a reservoir. As the path continues round to the right at this point, there is the remains of a sluice gate which once

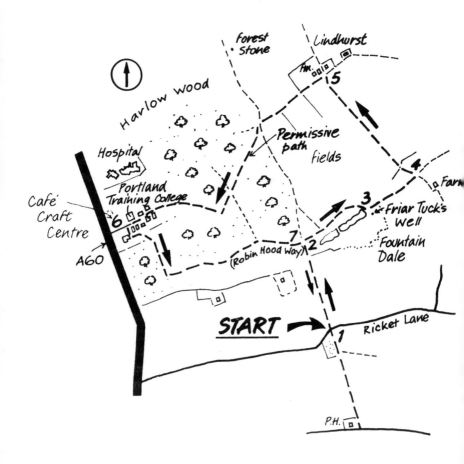

WALK 27

served the reservoir.

3. Where the path turns left to leave the wood, Friar Tuck's Well was located nearby in the trees. The path continues for about 530 metres to a junction of paths.

4. Turn left where the path crosses diagonally over a field into a grassy lane. Follow this lane to Lindhurst Farm.

5. Turn left, passing in front of the buildings along a wide, dirt lane leading to Harlow Wood. Continue straight on at the first junction, but turn left at the second junction. *You are now on a permissive path to create the Friar Tuck Trail.* Continue along this path to the second path to the right, turning right but taking the left-hand of the two paths. After a short distance you reach the buildings at Portland Training College for the Disabled. Go round the barrier, which is to keep out horses, and continue through the Centre until you come to a car park on the right, just before you reach the main road. In the car park there is a Craft Shop, Cafe and toilets.

6. When leaving the car park take the covered walkway opposite, leaving Portland College by the barrier at the end of the linking accommodation and re-entering the wood. Go straight on at the first junction, but turn left at the second junction. This takes you into the path signposted as the Robin Hood's Way. It is a clearly marked and fairly wide path which you follow for about 1.3 km until you come to a junction where there is a wooden shelter on the right. Turn left and after 50 metres you enter the wood.

7. Turn right and leave Harlow Wood, retracing the route to Ricket Lane and the start of the walk.

POINTS OF INTEREST

Friar Tuck's Well stood on the parish boundary at Fountaindale. Nearby is the moated area where the Friar lived and had his famous encounter with Robin Hood.

Portland Training School - long established as a retraining centre for the disabled.

28. Will Scarlet Walk

A circular walk taking in the Druid Stones, a visit to Blidworth Church where Robin Hood's minstrel Will Scarlet is supposed to be buried. We link onto Friar Tuck countryside.

THE FACTS

Area:	Blidworth
Distance:	6 km (4 miles)
Duration:	2 hours
Maps Required:	OS Pathfinder 795 (SK 45/55) Sutton in Ashfield
	OS Landranger 120 Mansfield & Worksop
Bus/Train Link:	Mansfield
Terrain:	Pleasantly undulating, good underfoot
Starting Point:	Park on grass verge in Ricket Lane near the Robin Hood Scout Centre SK 565561
Refreshments:	Bird in Hand public house, Blidworth

THE ROUTE

1.   Take the footpath towards Fishpool between two plantations, on the same side of the road as the Scout Centre. At the end of the plantation follow the footpath sign on the left and go over a stile. This is the first of 19 stiles on this part of the route but it is very easy to follow the path! Follow the field edge, not the definitive line across the field. At the tenth stile you will see some standing stones on the left: these are the Druid Stones. The eighteenth stile takes you into what appears to be someone's garden, but just follow the path round the house and over a stile leading into Ricket Lane, Blidworth.

2.   *A short diversion may be made at this point by turning right to go to the Bird in Hand public house or to visit Blidworth Church and the grave of Will Scarlet.* Otherwise turn left on Ricket Lane for 60 metres and take a stile to the right following a footpath sign, and cross a field to the opposite side and walk down the far side of that field, going over a stile into the next field. Continue towards another stile **but do not go over it.** Turn left and take another stile some 50 metres further along the field. Follow the path going over 3 more stiles after which it passes through a gap in the hedge into a field.

3.   Strike out at one o'clock over the brow of the rising land, passing a small pond on the right over the hill. Make for a stile which is located just to the right of a biggish tree. Cross diagonally to the right to another stile and continue diagonally to the right to another stile. Continue along the footpath leaving by way of a gate on what is the last stile of the walk, should the gate be locked.

4.   Cross the lane into a bridleway opposite leading to Providence Farm. Keep to the left of the farm passing through two gates and some trees into a large field. Turn left and follow the path, keeping the trees on the left until you enter the wood near to where Fountain Dale House once stood. As the path bears right, Friar Tuck's Well was located to the left and was in the House grounds.

5.   Follow the path as it skirts the edge of the trees and where it begins to turn left you will see the remains of a sluice gate which was used when a small reservoir existed in that area, then as the path progresses further round to the left, there can be seen on the left the remains of a moat, legendary site of the encounter between Robin Hood and Friar Tuck.

6.   The first junction of footpaths marks the point of entry into Harlow Wood proper. Continue straight on, ignoring a right-hand path, until the next junction of paths and turn left, passing out of the wood into a bridleway between hedges. Follow this bridleway to Ricket Lane.

POINTS OF INTEREST

Blidworth:

The village existed before Domesday and was surrounded by forest. It is believed that Maid Marion lived here before her marriage to Robin Hood. In St. Mary's churchyard is the grave of Will Scarlet.

Blidworth became a framework knitting centre, with 35 frames in use at one time. James Prior wrote *Forest Folk*, which he based in Blidworth and the Luddite frame-breaking which occurred in the village. In 1925 Blidworth pit was sunk, changing the village's fortunes once more.

The Druid Stones are the remains from the glacial age. In the past, children were passed through the hole in the stones to cure them of whooping cough.

Rocking Baby Ceremony is at least 400 years old and is performed at St. Mary's Church to commemorate the Presentation of Christ at the Temple. The male child born in Blidworth Parish nearest to Christmas Day is rocked in a beautiful flower-decked cradle at a special service on the first Sunday in February.

Fountaindale House was an early 19th century secluded house. Friar Tuck's Well stood at the boundary with Fountaindale.

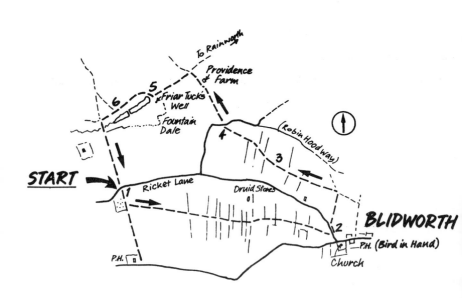

WALK 28

29. Roman Settlement of Farnsfield

A delightful circular walk taking in the Roman settlement of Combs Hill and going along beautiful Rob Lane, an ancient highway. Good views on this walk.

THE FACTS

Area:	Farnsfield
Distance:	7 km (4.25 miles) or 11 km (6.75 miles) with option
Duration:	2.5 hours without option: 3.5 hours with option
Maps Required:	OS Pathfinder 796 (SK 65/75) Newark West
	OS Landranger 120 Mansfield & Worksop
Bus/Train Link:	Southwell
Terrain:	Woods, farmland and tracks, a little hilly, some sections muddy
Starting Point:	St. Michael's Church, Farnsfield SK 646565
Refreshments:	Public houses, at Farnsfield

THE ROUTE

1.   From St. Michael's Church, walk towards the crossroad opposite Red Lion public house. Turn left down Blidworth Road and take footpath at the side of the wall to The Hall and new properties.

2.   Forward through double gates to cross two fields, half-left to enter a hedged track. In 200 metres veer right at a T-junction and after just over 1 km, 80 metres before the track bends right, turn half-left across an arable field to enter Combs Wood, seen ahead.

3.   Just inside the Wood follow the path to the right, then as you leave the trees,

walk up the hill to the right of the wood to join a hedged cart track (Rob Lane). Turn left.

4.   After 200 metres, at a footpath sign, the walker has the option to make a short detour to Robin Hood Hill, one of the finest viewpoints in Nottinghamshire.

If the option is taken, turn right, follow the hedge line for 300 metres, bear left and at the gap in the hedge go right for 150 metres to footpath sign, where you turn left to meet a minor road. Cross to the gate opposite, following the track until it bears left, then half-right at the foot of a copse. Follow the field edge path, keeping the trees on your left, to reach a stile. Over this, ascend half-left to the summit to enjoy the view.

To return to the main route, just retrace your steps to the footpath sign on Rob Lane (point 4).

5.   If coming from Robin Hood Hill turn right, or if this option is not taken, keep straight along Rob Lane to arrive at a track coming in from the left. Ignore this, turn right and go into a sunken path to reach the road opposite Wood Farm.

6.   Turn left along Greaves Lane and in 400 metres turn left again opposite Meadow Farm. We now leave the Robin Hood Way on a footpath, pass through a gate and forward for 100 metres, then turn right in the next field to the corner where you turn left keeping the hedge on your right. After 50 metres go through a gap in the hedge, turn left and ascend the hill now with the hedge on your left. At the top of the field follow the hedge to the right and in 200 metres turn left, as way-marked, through another opening.

7.   Walk downhill, with Farnsfield in the distance, continuing straight ahead to climb slightly to a stile. Continue in the same direction across another field to a stile which gives access to a newly-set plantation. Take the clear path between the trees forking right to enter Farnsfield Football Club ground via a gate.

8.   Walk down the left-hand side of the pitch, passing the changing rooms, to join a track. Where this turns left, take the stile on the right and continue with the hedge on the right to the end of the meadow. Turn right over a stile to enter a hedged twitchell which leads onto the main road opposite the Plough public house in Farnsfield.

9.   Turn left along Main Street to return to St. Michael's Church and the end of the walk.

POINTS OF INTEREST

Farnsfield:

This area has traces of ancient Roman camps, in particular at Combs Farm, and the ghost of a Roman soldier has reputedly been seen in local hostelries! Camp Hill was the site of an Iron Age earthwork.

It was also the birth-place of Augustus Charles Gregory, who emigrated to Australia and was the first man to explore the interior of the continent, becoming known as the Protector of the Aborigines.

The Parish Church is dedicated to St. Michael.

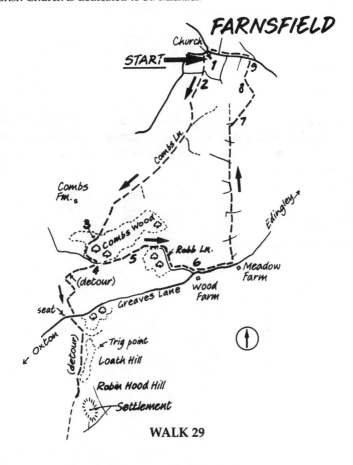

WALK 29

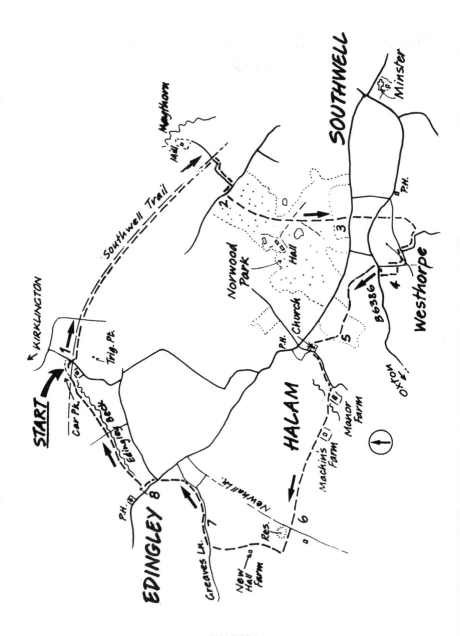

WALK 30

30. Norwood Hall: and the Bramley Apple

A recommended walk through Norwood Park, with its stately home and extensive orchards and some quiet and attractive villages.

THE FACTS

Area:	Kirklington, Halam, Edingley
Distance:	11.5 km (7.25 miles)
Duration:	3.5 hours
Maps Required:	OS Pathfinder 796 (SK 65/75) Newark West
	OS Landranger 120 Mansfield & Worksop
Bus/Train Link:	Southwell
Terrain:	Tracks and field paths
Starting Point:	Kirklington Station, Southwell Trail SK 675566
Refreshments:	Admiral Nelson, Westhorpe; public houses in Southwell; Old Reindeer public house, Edingley

THE ROUTE

1.   From the car park, follow the Trail past the former Station House and continue towards Southwell. After about 2 km you reach a road crossing the track. This leads to Maythorne. Our route turns right along a minor road to reach a main road. Turn right for 100 metres, then turn left to enter the grounds of Norwood Park.

2.   Follow the track into the Park to arrive at a crossroad junction. Go over the stile to follow a wide grass track. You have a beautiful view of Norwood House. On reaching the Halam Road cross it to enter a field opposite. Head across the field aiming just to the right of a brick house seen ahead.

3. On reaching the B6386, if you need refreshments turn left and walk to the Admiral Nelson public house seen just down the road. Our route continues across the road to enter a twitchell which leads to Westhorpe. Cross the road half-right to go up a second twitchell which leads to a small paddock. Cross the bridge and go right to a kissing gate. Pass through a group of attractive houses to a road, turning right and going round the corner to cross the field to the left.

4. Turn right to rejoin the road going uphill to reach the B6386. Follow the road opposite (Saversick Lane) past some ancient willows. You are now joining the Robin Hood Way. Turn left into the drive of the first house reached called Halam Gate'. Follow the fence on the left through the garden, over a stile into an orchard. Walk straight across the field to reach another stile.

5. Cross the stile, turn right and drop down into Halam to visit the church and have refreshments. Walk back up the lane (Radley Road) past the church and walk up to a path just short of the left hand bend in the road and Manor Farm. Take the path on the right which goes behind Manor Farm and past the tennis courts to a footbridge. Cross two stiles then turn right uphill past Machin's Farm. Continue straight ahead along the edge of fields to reach a lane.

6. Cross Newhall Lane and continue ahead up Turncroft Lane. After 200 metres take a path on the right and follow the edge of two fields passing New Hall Farm. This is the highest part of the walk with excellent views. Continue downhill through the remains of an orchard to reach Greaves Lane.

7. Turn right along Greaves Lane for 1 km to reach a field gate on the left just after the road junction on the right. Cross two fields, then go through a cottage garden to reach Edingley Main Street. Turn left past a road junction to reach a footpath on the right just before the village church and the Old Reindeer public house (some 100 metres away).

8. The path follows Edingley Beck over several fields to reach the Southwell Trail. Turn right on the track to reach the car park.

POINTS OF INTEREST

Kirklington:

The church of St. Swithin is partly Norman. The pulpit has holes in it, which have been filled. Apparently early in the 19th century, the sporting rector used to take he pulpit, which was loose from its base, down on weekdays to shoot wild duck, using the pulpit as a screen. The holes were to enable him to fire through them at the birds!

There are many old customs associated with the village, such as the *Kirklington Feast* held on the first Sunday in October, when all sons and daughters working away from home, married or in service, went home for Feast Sunday. Two stalls were set up in front of the Whetham Arms (now Ivy Farm House) on Saturday evening and did a good trade in sweets, oranges, brandy snap and gingerbread. Another custom was to ring the treble bell every Sunday morning at 8.00am, whether there was an early service or not, and also at 11.00am on Shrove Tuesday, to warn housewives to begin cooking their pancakes.

Halam:

The church, dedicated to St. Michael the Archangel, is a Norman chantry chapel of Southwell Minster. Local tradition believes that the church was built from stone removed from carts hauling the stone destined for Southwell to build the Minster, as the carts waited at the foot of Halam Hill for extra horses to pull them up.

Edingley:

The church is dedicated to St. Giles, and has been much altered, with the south aisle demolished, along with a tower. In the north wall one Norman window remains, as narrow as an arrow slit.

Norwood Park and House:

Home of Sir John and Lady Victoria Starkey.

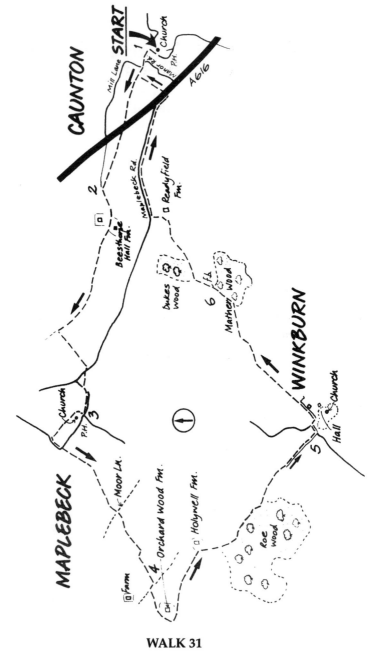

WALK 31

31. There's No Honey In This Beehive, Just Beer!

A gentle ramble around a quiet corner of Nottinghamshire giving the opportunity to quench your thirst in the smallest pub in the county and passing two country manor houses - Winkburn and Beesthorpe.

THE FACTS

Area:	Caunton, Maplebeck, Winkburn
Distance:	13 km (8 miles)
Duration:	4 hours
Maps Required:	OS Pathfinder 796 (SK 65/75) Newark West and 780 (SK 66/76) Ollerton
	OS Landranger 120 Mansfield & Worksop
Bus/Train Link:	Newark
Terrain:	Field paths and tracks, some arable fields
Starting Point:	Caunton Church SK 745601
Refreshments:	The Plough, Caunton; The Beehive, Maplebeck
Please note:	This is a very attractive walk, but we do have some definitive line path problems on the route. We describe the definitive line throughout the walk, but in paragraph 4 (Orchard Wood Farm) we describe a permissive route. In other parts of the walk, field boundaries have been removed. We shall endeavour to have the definitive line properly reinstated and the route fully way-marked.

THE ROUTE

1.   Walk past the Plough, turn left into Mill Lane and forward to a right-hand bend to cross the stile ahead. Cross two paddocks. Keep the hedge on your right and continue to the A616. Cross to the gate opposite, then bear right to a track which leads to Beesthorpe Hall.

2.   Go around the left-hand side of the Hall following the way-marks through the garden to a stile. Turn right along a track and forward when it bends right, to the corner of a field. Follow the edge of two fields, go through the gate left, then turn right and go round two sides of the field. Cross the Beck and forward to the minor road. Turn right for 20 metres, cross the stile left and go diagonally right to a gate. Turn left to walk through Maplebeck to the Church.

3.   The Beehive is just beyond, but our route follows the lane to the right of the Church and past a gravel drive. Don't cross the stream instead walk forward to join a road. Turn left and at the corner turn right through the gateway of Brecks Farm. Turn immediately left to cross a vast field aiming just to the right of a pylon, then walk forward to meet the remnants of Moor Lane. Cross the fence, go half-right to the electricity posts then follow the track across four fields to a road.

4.   Turn right, then left to Orchard Wood Farm and left again just beyond the farmhouse, along the edge of a field. *Please note the definitive line is* **not** *possible.* Please walk the permissive route as signposted (see note above). Continue ahead in two fields to emerge near Holywell Farm, then walk forward following a hedge then veer right to the northern tip of Roe Wood. Turn left to follow a track alongside the wood to reach Winkburn.

5.   At the road turn left and in 100 metres turn right at the junction to follow a track which bears left before the Church. Follow the hedge right for 500 metres then veer right across a field, passing under power lines, to a gap in the hedge. Through the gap turn left and in 300 metres cross diagonally right to Mather Wood. Keep the wood on your right, walk over a footbridge, to follow a hedge left to the south east corner of Dukes Wood. Cross the large field half-left to meet the access drive of Readyfield Farm and the road.

6.   Turn right and after 1 km cross the A616 then right and take the large stile, left, reached via a lay-by. Cross to the cricket field and go around it to pass tennis courts and to emerge onto the road. Forward along Manor Road to the Church.

POINTS OF INTEREST

Caunton:

This village is well worth exploring since it possesses a ford, a disused windmill and a lovely beck-side footpath which is frequently crossed by the local duck population. The church of St. Andrew dates from 1200, and was restored in the 19th century.

Caunton Manor was built early in the 18th century and extended this century. Caunton is the village of the man Tennyson called "The Rose King": Samuel Reynolds Hole, who lived at Caunton Manor as vicar and squire before serving as Dean of Rochester. He studied roses and became a famous amateur rose grower. In 1851 he had 1,027 trees with over 400 varieties.

Maplebeck:

A picturesque hamlet, again is well worth exploring, but not before taking refreshment at the quaint Beehive Inn. The parish church is dedicated to St. Radegund.

Winkburn:

The church, dedicated to St. John of Jerusalem, has an undisturbed Georgian interior with box pews, a Jacobean pulpit and a rare 17th century arched screen. The adjacent Hall dates from the early 18th century whilst its ownership has now reverted back to the Craven-Smith-Milnes family, who have undertaken to restore the old Hall to its former glory.

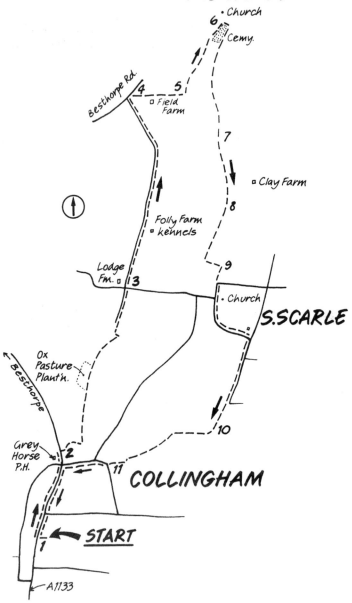

WALK 32

32. Collingham and the Scarles

This walk links the villages of Collingham, North Scarle and South Scarle, following field edge paths, tracks and a few sections of road.

THE FACTS

Area:	Collingham, North Scarle, South Scarle
Distance:	13 km (8 miles)
Duration:	4 hours
Maps Required:	OS Pathfinder 781 (SK 86/96) Lincoln South
	OS Landranger 121 Lincoln
Bus/Train Link:	Newark
Terrain:	Very easy, flat paths and tracks, but muddy south of North Scarle
Starting Point:	Collingham Health Centre SK 831617
Refreshments:	Three public houses in Collingham; White Hart pub, North Scarle

THE ROUTE

1.   Leave the car park to join the High Street and proceed northwards until you reach the Grey Horse pub, on the left of the main road.

2.   Just beyond the pub locate a stile on the right hand side of the road. Enter the field, turn right to the brook and follow this until just past a stand of poplars. Turn left here, following the Trent Valley Way marker and continue ahead to the field corner, where you maintain direction towards the right hand side of Ox Pasture Plantation. Follow the way-markers through the right hand side of the copse to a field edge path over two fields. At the field corner turn left for 75 metres before turning right onto a track leading to a road.

3.   Cross straight over the road with Lodge Farm on your left and follow the lane (Meer Lane becoming Felly Lane) for 2 km until just before Besthorpe Road.

4.   Here turn right past Field Farm and continue on farm track to the hedge corner where you turn sharp left following a way marker.

5.   Follow the hedge until a stile on your left leads into a meadow. Walk ahead, first with the willows and hawthorn on your right, and cross the field to a stile, then across two more meadows. In the next field, angle to a finger-post and stile in the right-hand corner.

6.   Enter the cemetery, turn left to the metal gates. *At this point, you could continue through North Scarle to the White Hart Inn. Otherwise,* turn right in front of the gates and pass through a gap in the fence on the far side of the cemetery. Turn right immediately and, with the cemetery now on your right, head away from North Scarle.

7.   Enter a cultivated field keeping the hedge on your right and when the hedge turns sharp right, keep straight ahead aiming for a small, raised grassy mound ahead. There is no obvious path here, but follow a raised grassy bank aiming to the right of the large farm buildings in the distance. When the grassy bank turns left, keep ahead over a small earth bridge to a farm track where you follow yellow way-markers at a field corner. Follow the field side with the hedge on your right and cross into another field through a gap in the hedge next to yellow way-markers, which lead ahead towards two oak trees at the field corner. Here cross the ditch by planks and, aiming to the right of two large trees, continue ahead at the field corner but with the hedge now on your right.

8.   Maintain direction towards South Scarle ignoring way-markers on the right from Holly House Farm, and at the next field corner turn left.

9.   When the hedge turns right follow it to enter South Scarle between houses with a tall, evergreen hedge on your left. At the road continue ahead past the church and the Hall on your left. Follow the road around to the left and at a T-junction turn right along a road that soon becomes a farm track.

10.   At the track end turn right over ditchboards and, after following the field edge path with a ditch on your left, turn left at a finger post to join and turn right onto a wide track which leads to large metal barriers.

11.   Keep straight ahead following Woodhill Road until you reach the High Street in Collingham, with the Grey Horse pub opposite. Turn left here and retrace your steps to the car park.

POINTS OF INTEREST

Collingham:

The separate parishes of North and South Collingham have united to form one long, leafy, riverside village. The two churches serving these joined parishes are All Saints Church in North Collingham and St. John the Baptist Church in South Collingham. The River Trent is almost 2 km from Collingham, but the stones by the gate in the churchyard wall indicate floods badly affected the village in 1795, 1875 and 1947. North Collingham had a village cross, of which the base and lower part of the shaft survive and are to be found north-east of All Saints Church. The remains indicate that the cross must have been of great size.

South Scarle:

Parish church dedicated to St. Helen, which has a Medieval exterior and Norman interior.

Church Farmhouse stands to the south of the Church and boasts a 17th century shaped gable.

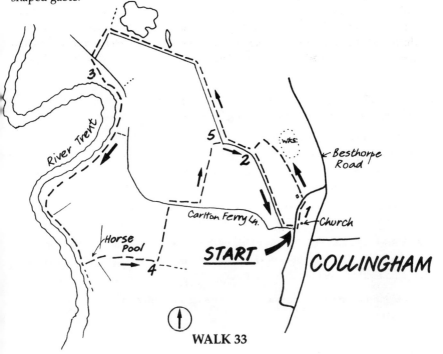

WALK 33

33. Collingham Lake District

An easy walk through the lakelands of Collingham passing the ancient Horse Pool to follow part of the Trent Valley Way, Nottinghamshire County Council's long distance route which runs from Thrumpton to West Stockwith.

THE FACTS

Area:	Collingham
Distance:	8 km (5 miles)
Duration:	2.5 hours
Maps Required:	OS Pathfinder 781 (SK 86/96) Lincoln South
	OS Landranger 121 Lincoln
Bus/Train Link:	Newark
Terrain:	Field tracks and paths, easy walking
Starting Point:	North Collingham Church SK 829620
Refreshments:	Three pubs in Collingham

THE ROUTE

1.   From the church in Low Street walk north for 300 metres to enter the twitchell on the left between houses. At the end turn right over the stream and through the farm gate into a grass field. Follow the hedge right for 250 metres then veer left to a footbridge. Over this, cross an arable field to come out onto North Croft Lane.

2.   Turn right and in 300 metres fork right to follow this wide lane for 2 km to a T-junction. Turn left and at the next junction go ahead to the stile opposite. Cross the field half-left to meet the River Trent towpath.

3.   Continue on top of the floodbank, passing a recently built house, for 2 km to a

fishermen's car park. Leave the towpath by the stile at a footpath sign immediately after the car park. The path bears left after a few metres, to meet a clear track. Follow this for 500 metres, passing Horse Pool on your left, to a track on the left.

4.   Take the track for 500 metres and at the end turn right into Carlton Ferry Lane. After 300 metres turn left alongside Ferry Lane Farm to emerge back onto Northcroft Lane.

5.   Turn right along the wide grassy track for 1 km to its junction with the minor road, then left to the church.

POINTS OF INTEREST

Collingham:

The separate parishes of North and South Collingham have united to form one long, leafy, riverside village. The two churches serving these joined parishes are All Saints Church in North Collingham and St. John the Baptist Church in South Collingham. The River Trent is almost 2 km from Collingham, but as you see from the stones by the gate in the churchyard wall, floods badly affected the village in 1795, 1875 and 1947. North Collingham had a village cross, of which the base and lower part of the shaft survive and are to be found north-east of All Saints Church. The remains indicate that the cross must have been of great size.

Much of the land between the river and the village has suffered from over-enthusiastic sand and gravel extraction in the past. However, parts are now being restored to nature reserves as can be seen by the signs in the region of **Mons Pool**.

Horse Pool on Westfield Lane was once used by the local farm horses to quench their thirst.

34. The Wood and Moor of Stapleford

This walk will take you from the north of Stapleford Wood to the Danish settlement on the top of Danethorpe Hill and then to the site of Crococalana: a Roman settlement on the Fosse Way.

THE FACTS

Area:	Stapleford, near Newark; Brough
Distance:	11 km (6.5 miles)
Duration:	3.5 hours
Maps Required:	OS Pathfinder 797 (SK 85/95) Newark on Trent (East)
	OS Landranger 121 Lincoln
Bus/Train Link:	Newark
Terrain:	Rolling landscape to the east of the Fosse Way with forest tracks, headland paths and quiet roads
Starting Point:	Junction of Lodge Drive and Stapleford Lane SK 863573
Refreshments:	None

THE ROUTE

1.   Having parked your car near the junction of Lodge Drive and Coddington Lane cross the Lane and take the track that passes to the right of the house and leads through the wood, keeping straight ahead where the track bends to the left. At the end of the track, follow the finger post direction diagonally across to a field corner where you climb a stile and maintain your direction towards East Field Farm.

2.   Pass through a gateway and then immediately pass a wooden five-barred gate to join the farm track alongside farm buildings on your left. Proceed along the track, passing stables and a tennis court on your right, and then, having passed large corrugated farm buildings and pig houses, you will eventually come to a water tower on the right of the track which is by now metalled.

3.   Just beyond the next cottage turn right at a finger post, climb a stile into a paddock and head straight across towards Danethorpe Hill Farm. Having climbed another stile, maintain your direction across the lawn in front of the farmhouse making for the far left corner of a low pig house. Incline left here to the next way-marker at which point Brough comes into view, and continue ahead with a hedge on your right.

4.   When the hedge turns sharp left in front of you, pass through a gap in the hedge to cross ditchboards and turn right immediately to follow the field side with a hedge on your right. At the next corner turn left, still with a hedge on your right, to join the track that leads from Little Danethorpe Farm on your left. Continue ahead to join Norwell Lane where you turn left. Soon you will come to a finger post on the right of the lane that leads you across several stiles to meet the main road at Holly Farm.

5.   Turn right along the busy main road (A46*) until you reach the junction with Stapleford Lane, where you turn right and proceed past Corner Farm to the first house on your left.

   * Please note: this road is due to be upgraded in the very near future, so the description may vary slightly.

6.   Just before this house turn left at a finger post, head for the telegraph pole where you incline 45 to your right towards a single tree on the far side of the field and in line with Brills Hill Farm in the distance. On reaching the hedge, look for two boards across a ditch beyond a gap in the hedge and, maintaining your direction diagonally across the field, you will come to a minor road and then a bridge. Keep on the road uphill past Brills Hill Farm and then the poultry houses of Grove Farm. The road, which leads to Norton Disney, soon inclines to the right and soon after, just before a single house on the left, you turn right.

7.   This track, Thoroughfare Lane, leads you towards the northernmost stands of Stapleford Moor which you enter on its north eastern edge.

8.   **Just beyond** a fire break on your right, look for a right hand fork which you follow through the wood until you rejoin the road.

9.   Turn left on the road and at the crossroads, with a large tree gracing a grassy island, turn right. In 100 metres you will pass the wide drive to Moor Farm on your right, until you arrive at the junction of Coddington Lane and Lodge Drive, where your car will be waiting.

POINTS OF INTEREST

It may come as a surprise to find such views in "flat" Nottinghamshire as can be had from the highest point of this walk near Danethorpe Hill Farm.

Nothing much remains of the **Roman Settlement at Brough**, which was the site of the Roman roadside town of Crococalana, and which may have begun as a Roman fort in the middle of 1 AD. The village does have a tiny, unaisled church dating from 1885.

Stapleford Wood with its many rhododendron bushes, is now the site of twentieth century battles against industrialisation.

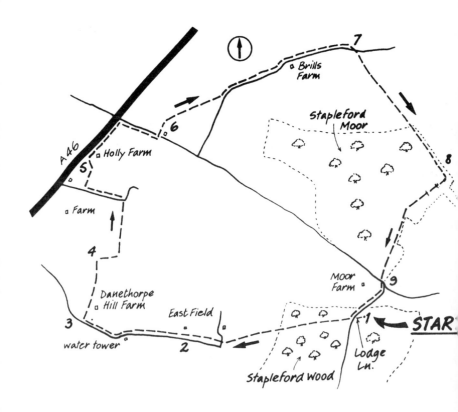

WALK 34

35. Balderton Lakeside

An easy walk, ideal for winter, since the walk is on good surfaces throughout the parish of Balderton and around the lake, the scene of many environmental improvements.

THE FACTS

Area: Balderton

Distance: 6 km (3.75 miles)

Duration: 1.75 hours

Maps Required: OS Pathfinder 797 (SK 85/95) Newark (East) & Navenby

                   OS Landranger 121 Lincoln

Bus/Train Link: Newark

Terrain: Easy village footways

Starting Point: St. Giles Church, Main Street, Balderton SK 820516

Refreshments: Numerous pubs in Balderton

THE ROUTE

1.   From the church cross the road into Bullpit Road and after 200 metres bear left into Macauley Drive, then left again into Warwick Road. Almost immediately take the twitchell right, alongside the Grove playing field, to emerge into Coronation Street.

2.   Turn left, and at the end left again onto London Road. In 100 metres cross right, into Rowan Way. Follow this road for 300 metres, then bear left into the Lakeside area.

3.   Walk to the right, on the perimeter path, eventually leaving it to bear right to emerge onto the bed of an old railway track. Although not a right of way, this is used regularly by the local dog walkers. Turn left and walk southwards for 900 metres then turn left, just past the engineering works, into Lowfield Lane.

117

4.   Follow this until you reach some cottages. At the last one turn left up a footpath and after 400 metres turn right at a T-junction. After 500 metres veer right, right through a play area to join Lowfield Lane where you bear left to emerge onto London Road.

5.   Cross over into Blind Lane, then forwards into Sykes Lane and veer left into Pinfold Lane, passing Pinfold Cottage right, to return to your starting point.

POINTS OF INTEREST

Balderton:

The *Lake*, a remnant of gravel extraction, has undergone extensive environmental improvements. This is due to the efforts of the local Parish Council, with assistance from the local Spadework project officers of Nottinghamshire County Council.

In the garden of **Pinfold Cottage** can be seen the remnants of the old village pinfold, used to keep stray animals in until their owners paid the Pinner money for their release.

The spire of *St. Giles* church dates from the 13th century, and their are examples of 14th and 16th century stained glass in the chancel windows.

Earthworks of the besieging Parliamentary Army in the Civil War once surrounded the village of Balderton, but these have now largely been destroyed.

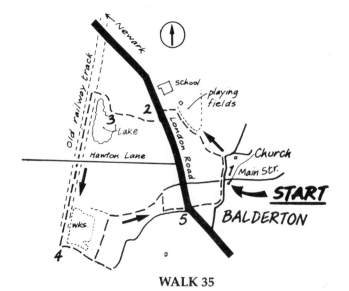

WALK 35

36. Willow Holt

A very popular riverside walk, often busy with fishermen, boaters and walkers.

THE FACTS

Area: Farndon

Distance: 6.5 km (4 miles)

Duration: 2 hours

Maps Required: OS Pathfinder 796 (SK 65/75) Newark on Trent (West)

                  OS Landranger 120 Mansfield & Worksop

Bus/Train Link: Newark

Terrain: Very easy, flat walk. No stiles.

Starting Point: Outside Lazy Otter public house, Farndon SK 768521

Refreshments: Lazy Otter public house, Farndon; Travellers' Rest, Farndon Road

THE ROUTE

1.   From the car park follow the riverside path with the River Trent on your left. Continue over Farndon Harbour Bridge.

2.   Continue following the loop of the Trent at Baggarley Rack, past Staythorpe Power Station on the opposite bank. At the weir (a favourite feeding spot for herons) the old Trent continues past Averham and Kelham to rejoin the main flow past Newark, but we follow the Newark Dyke, past the flower-rich hay meadows and fishermen's car park near the windmill.

3.   Continue through two clapper gates, past the disused windmill to join the riverside track. Under the new road bridge, continue past old maltings and houses. Follow the track away from the river to the main road.

4.   Turn right out of Dorner Avenue and follow the road (old Roman Fosse Road) towards Farndon. Pass the Travellers' Rest public house (not obligatory!) and a row of cottages. Turn right down a stony track, back to the riverside. Here you turn left, retracing your steps under the road bridge. Before the clapper gate, turn left up a passage between houses and a hedge and continue straight ahead into Farndon until you reach a crossroads and a mini-roundabout.

5.   Here you turn right down a track for 200 metres. Turn left and continue with an unfenced field on your right. Where the track turns right, keep straight on, following the path through a grassy area, with the marina on your right, passing a wildflower meadow. Continue and pass some lock-up garages and walk on down the road (North End) to the road junction.

6.   At the road end, turn left. After 70 metres follow the footpath to the right between houses to Chapel Lane. Here you turn right, then immediately left, following the track and crossing Church Street to walk up by Farndon parish church. Continue past the church, and turn left through the church gate. Turn right at the road junction and walk to a pleasant country lane (Wykes Lane). Here turn right and follow the lane back to the start, passing the restored retting ponds in the meadows on the left, which form part of the Willowholt Nature Reserve.

POINTS OF INTEREST

This walk provides much of interest to the naturalist. Numerous water birds can be found along the riverside; great-crested grebe, mallard, tufted duck, moorhen, coot, Canada geese and swans are common. Herons are always in evidence, and the spectacular kingfisher is often seen. There is also a wide variety of aquatic plants around the riverbank, including purple loosestrife, marsh woundwort, yellow water lily and arrowhead; whilst the lush water meadows include ladysmock, greater turnet and meadow cranesbill. The marina ponds are alive with willow warblers in the spring and the colourful yellow wagtail breeds in the riverside fields.

Farndon:

St. Peter's Church. A Viking sword was found in the churchyard, which is one of the few objects of Danish origin from the county.

The area had a tradition of farming, malting, willow growing and basket making: Mr. Lever Howitt, a wealthy conservationist, left his estate, *Willow Holts* to the National Trust. Other reminders of this craft may be found in the willow trees and retting ponds.

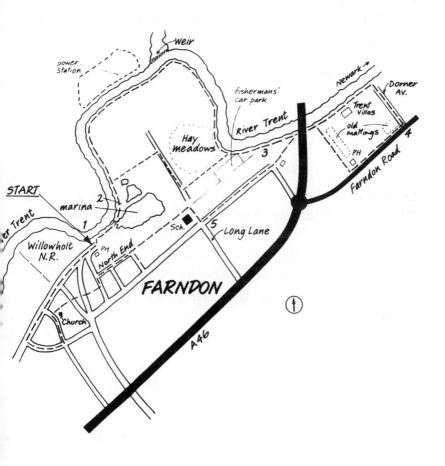

WALK 36

37. Horses Galore!

A pleasant country walk following field paths and country lanes over typical central Nottinghamshire farming countryside, crossing Southwell racecourse.

THE FACTS

Area:	Rolleston, Upton
Distance:	8 km (5 miles)
Duration:	2.5 hours
Maps Required:	OS Pathfinder 796 (SK 65/75) Newark on Trent (West)
	OS Landranger 120 Mansfield & Worksop
Bus/Train Link:	Newark
Terrain:	Generally flat. Field paths, track and country lanes. Ten stiles to negotiate. Can be muddy in places in winter.
Starting Point:	Outside Rolleston Church SK 742525 or the first Racecourse car park on the right, just past the church
Refreshments:	None en route. Available in Upton and Southwell

THE ROUTE

1.   From the church walk out of the village towards Southwell Racecourse. Cross the Racecourse car park on the right, just past the church (ignoring directions to the public car park). Go over the railway line and bear right to Rolleston Mill.

2.   Turn left (signposted Trent Valley Way) between the Mill and outbuildings and cross the stile, ignoring the bridge which goes back to the Racecourse. Continue ahead through the golf course (watch out for golf balls!) with the River Greet and Southwell Racecourse on the left. Continue over the bridge by a concrete overflow (ignore footpath to the right) and follow the river round to the left.

3. After 300 metres at the signpost (Trent Valley Way) turn right across the field keeping to the right of the hedge. Halfway along the hedge, take the stile to the left and continue diagonally left across a cropped field. Cross a concrete bridge over the stream into a green lane. Here there are good views of Upton Church and Upton Hall between the trees.

4. Go left along the green lane to the end *(a footpath on the right leads to Upton for refreshment and a visit to the Church)*. Turn left onto the road towards Upton Mill. Immediately after crossing the bridge, cross a stile on the right, go diagonally left to the double stile in the field corner. Follow the River Greet on your left until you reach a footbridge.

5. Cross the bridge and continue with the river on your right. Where a mature field hedge comes down to the river, pass through the gap and follow the hedge away from the river, keeping to the right of the hedge. The route continues along the top of the long field, parallel to the old railway line (now a supply road to Southwell Racecourse). Cross the stile and a footbridge, then go through a gate on the left. Over the road and a stile opposite into a field. Continue right to a stile under a pylon in the hedge. Over the stile and follow the left hand hedge round to the stile and enter Crewe Lane. *(At this point a right turn will lead you into Southwell.)*

6. Turn left and follow the lane, passing Dale Farm on the left. Pass through a gap by a metal gate (here there are good views of Upton village and beyond). Continue down the track, passing sewage works and a house on the left. Follow the path until you reach the service road to the refuse tip. Turn right, go along the road to a stile on the left of the main gates (the gates are often locked). Turn left at the main road and go over the old railway bridge.

7. 100 metres over the bridge take the footpath to left over a stile. **Extreme care** is needed here as there is a steep, stepped descent down the path. Continue along a well-defined path, over footbridges and follow Beck Dyke on your right to a playing field. Go onto the road and follow the road, across the railway line, back to the start point.

POINTS OF INTEREST

Diversions may be made to visit:-

Upton: which has two good public houses; the church of St. Peter whose tower was also intended to be used as a dovecote; and **Upton Hall**, built c1830, which is now the Headquarters of the British Horological Institute, whose exhibition of clocks and timepieces is open to the public on summer Sundays and Bank Holidays

Southwell: a charming, historic town with its splendid Minster, the Mother Church for Nottinghamshire, including the wonderful Chapter House and interesting Minster Close. Also the **Saracen's Head Hotel**, the oldest inn in Southwell, where Charles I stayed prior to his surrender in 1646.

There are 18th and 19th century cottages in the town, including the site where the first Bramley Apple was grown, now a museum.

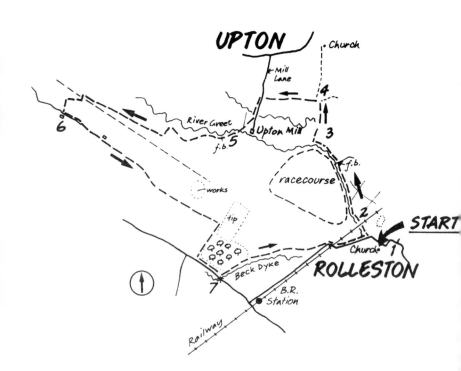

WALK 37

38. Rev. William Lee Walk

A circular walk taking in Ramsdale House, former home of the Seely family, two Iron Age forts (Cockpit Hill and Foxhill), through Watchwood Plantation, Oxton Bogs, Oxton Village to Calverton, home of the Rev. William Lee, inventor of the stocking frame and the Roietes, a religious cult.

THE FACTS

Area:	Oxton, Calverton
Distance:	15 km (9 miles)
Duration:	4.5 hours
Maps Required:	OS Pathfinder 795 (SK 45/55) Sutton in Ashfield, 796 (SK 65/75) Newark on Trent (West), 812 (SK 44/54) Nottingham (North) & Ilkeston, 813 (SK 64/74) Carlton & Elston
	OS Landranger 120 Mansfield and Worksop and OS 129 Nottingham & Loughborough
Bus/Train Link:	Calverton
Terrain:	Woodland and field paths
Starting Point:	Small car park at the junction of Spindle Lane Bridleway and Georges Lane, Calverton SK 602484
Refreshments:	Green Dragon, Ye Bridge Inn and the Post Office at Oxton; numerous shops and public houses in Calverton.

THE ROUTE

1.   With the bridleway at your back, face on-coming traffic and walk westwards along Georges Lane as far as the bend, turn right along a track. On approaching houses veer right along a track as far as a stile, go over and left alongside the hedge

at the side of the golf course, until you reach the wood. This is the site of Cockpit Hill, an Iron Age fort. Turn right and walk downhill towards the house in the hollow (Hollinwood House), climb the stile and keep to the left of the house and continue down to the road. At the road turn left, walk to the crossroads, and keep on until you meet a track on the right going towards Calverton Colliery.

2.   Leave the road here and enter the field, following the path with the hedge on your left. On reaching the wood, turn right to its edge for about 170 metres, turn left and follow a straight path for about 450 metres, turn right along a grass path until you go under power lines, then continue straight along a track until a path leaves on the left about 75 metres before a white triangulation pillar.

3.   Take this path which soon joins a green track, walk right uphill along the track until it rejoins our original path a few metres to the left of the triangulation pillar. Go left and follow the path until it bends sharply to the right, then bear half-right on the bend to come to the edge of the wood. Walk right as far as a public footpath sign by a hedge on the left, and then turn left alongside the hedge, heading away from the wood. At the bottom, turn right parallel to the railway line which here runs through a Bunter Sandstone cutting.

4.   On meeting the next hedge turn left and over the line to the junction of Salterford and Whinbush Lanes. Head for the gate opposite and go down the farm track for 15 metres. Look over the field to your right, we cross this field half-right, ie about 45 from the track heading a little to the left of the right-hand end of a wood on the hillside in front of you. Once over the brow of the field you look for a way-marked post in the fence, through this and follow the path to cross a section of ground separating dammed sections of the Dover Beck in an area called Oxton Bogs.

5.   As you leave this wooded area over thick, timber ditchboards, you meet a junction of farm tracks, walk straight on alongside a fence towards the left side of a wood, taking the track heading half-right uphill. At the top turn half-left alongside the hedge. At the track junction continue to the road, crossing the road **with care** to the gate opposite and following the track to meet Forest Road. Then turn right into Oxton village.

6.   Continue past the Church to turn left down New Road, and soon you meet a delightful ford. Don't cross it, but walk right alongside the stream aptly named Water Lane. At the end walk straight, past Ye Bridge Inn, to a traffic island. Cross

with care over the road to again follow the stream alongside a path. Stay with the stream until it turns left. We follow the path to the side of a wood, and continue on the path close to the wood to reach Woodview Farm and Mansfield Lane.

7.   Turn left and walk to Carrington Lane. Walk down this narrow country lane for 130 metres to join Crookdole Lane at a bend in the road by the side of a new housing estate. Turn right up Crookdole Lane, then take the path to the left after 50 metres, going over a culvert bridge and along a twitchell to reach a cul-de-sac, then carrying straight ahead to Moor Road. Walk down this to its end to join Bonner Lane. Turn right and walk past The Gleaners public house then Windles Square (a row of framework knitters' cottages), then along Main Street, past Calverton House to arrive at St. Wilfred's Church. *(You can continue to Mansfield Lane to a William Lee Interpretation Board opposite St. Wilfred's Square or visit the Calverton Folk Museum at the side of the Baptist Church on Main Street).*

8.   From St. Wilfred's Church, cross the road to Burner Pool, follow the road and where it divides take the right fork to reach a stile on the left at the next bend. Turn right which brings you onto Bricknell Road. Walk up the road and turn right up the twitchell to reach an open space. Turn half-left to a fence to enter a field. Take the path that climbs uphill to reach a bridleway (Spindle Lane) at the top of the large field.

9.   Turn right and walk along Spindle Lane for 1.8km to reach the end of our walk. Take the time to enjoy the view along this green lane.

POINTS OF INTEREST

Calverton:

This was the centre of the framework knitting industry, and there are many examples of stocking-knitters' cottages, for example in Windle Square.

St. Wilfred's Church has Norman panels showing St. Wilfred, Bishop of York, giving blessings after baptism, together with panels of the rural occupations throughout the year.

Calverton Folk Museum, Main Street, is housed in stockingers' cottages dating from 1780. Calverton was the home of Rev. William Lee, who invented the stocking frame.

Oxton:

The church of St. Peter has a blocked Norman doorway, and a rare pillar piscina.

Oxton Hall was the seat of the Sherbrooke family, but was demolished in 1957. A stuccoed stable survives and the tomb of Robert Sherbrooke, who died in 1710, may be found close to the lane, surrounded by iron railings.

Foxwood an ancient British encampment.

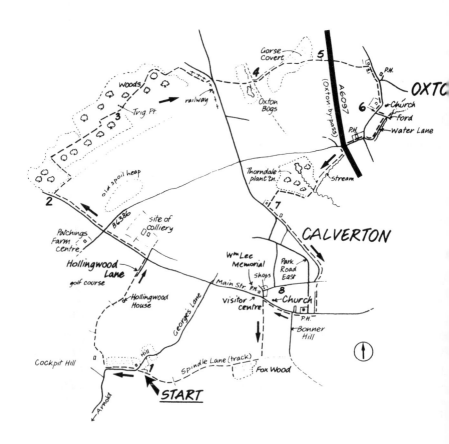

WALK 38

39. Nell Gwynne's Best Woods For Hunting and Walking

See if you agree with Nell Gwynne, paramour of Charles II, who enjoyed her stay at the Royal Hunting Lodge and thought these were the "best woods" for walking.

THE FACTS

Area:	Bestwood
Distance:	8 km (5 miles)
Duration:	2.5 hours
Maps Required:	OS Pathfinder 812 (SK 44/54) Nottingham North and Ilkeston
	OS Landranger 121 Lincoln
Bus/Train Link:	Bulwell
Terrain:	Well defined paths, easy walking, although a little hilly
Starting Point:	Car Park of the Old Winding House, Park Road, Bestwood Village SK 556475
Refreshments:	Bestwood Village

THE ROUTE

1.   Leave the car park and turn right along Park Road. After 400 metres take the footpath on the left. Follow this path over two fields, over a stile. Proceed along the path with houses on your left, eventually reaching a field where you drop down to a footpath sign. Turn right, following through to emerge onto a road. Walk across an open space, and continue along The Spinney until you meet the Moor Road B683.

2.   Take the road opposite and follow the signpost for mill lakes. Ignore the first gate, but continue until you cross the River Leen. Turn left, go through a gate to reach the mill lakes. Take the well-defined path round the lake, going once again over a bridge and the River Leen. Take the path straight on to drop down the steps and once again reach Moor Road (B683).

3.   Take the path opposite and climb up to an old railway embankment. Follow the cinder track for 400 metres until you reach a junction of hardcore paths.

4.   Turn left and go through a gate. You are now in Bestwood Country Park. Proceed directly up on the well-defined hardcore path which climbs steeply. Observe the view when at the top.

5.   Follow the path round to the right and continue down until reaching a crossroads of paths. Take the path on the left, and keep the houses of Rise Park on your immediate right. Follow this tree-lined path for 500 metres.

6.   On reaching the sign Bigwood 5 mins turn left to follow the winding path downhill, at the sign Alexandra Lodge 15 mins turn right and walk until you reach the sign Woodman's Path'. At this point, turn left, follow this path past the play park on your right and on past the toilet block, reaching a tarmac path. Observe on your right Alexandra Lodge.

7.   After viewing the Lodge, return along the wide tarmac path, through the barred gate and onto the road, eventually reaching the Old Winding House Car Park on your left.

POINTS OF INTEREST

Bestwood:

The village lies in the area which once formed part of the Royal Hunting Park of Bestwood. The Plantagenet kings were first to hunt here, and built the first Bestwood Lodge. Richard III was staying here when he received the message that Henry Tudor had mounted his invasion, which led to the Battle of Bosworth Field and the loss of Richard's crown and life.

According to legend, King Charles II hunted here with Nell Gwynne and he promised her all the land she could ride around before breakfast. As she was not noted for being an early riser, he felt his estates were safe. However, she got up at dawn and rode around the estate, dropping handkerchiefs along the way.

Certainly she did own the land and her son by Charles became the first Duke of St. Albans.

As the area become more industrialised, two cotton mills were built on the river Leen and coalmining and ironworks became established.

Bestwood Park:The present Bestwood Lodge is an Hotel, standing in the Bestwood Country Park, which is open for pleasant walks.

Alexandra Lodge was built between 1858 and 1877.

WALK 39

40. The Three Mills

Discover three beautiful old water mills on the Dover Beck, a tributory of the Trent, in a tranquil part of the county. One of the mills has a particularly unsavoury history, as you will find out later.

THE FACTS

Area:	Lowdham, Gonalston
Distance:	6 km (4 miles)
Duration:	2 hours
Maps Required:	OS Pathfinder 813 (SK 64/74) Carlton & Elston
	OS Landranger 129 Nottingham & Loughborough
Bus/Train Link:	Nottingham
Terrain:	Easy field paths, can be muddy after rain.
Starting Point:	Lowdham Church SK 663468
Refreshments:	Numerous pubs in Lowdham

THE ROUTE

1.   From the parking area ascend past the Church and take the path right which leads to a field. Keeping the hedge on your right, forward to join an access road. Turn right to the A6097 which you cross **with care** half-left to enter the access drive of Lowdham Mill. Just before the Mill, fork right through a handgate and an orchard, and pass to the right of the buildings to eventually meet Gonalston Lane.

2.   Turn right for 1 km to take a footpath sign and stile right. Cross the field half-left, to the right of a cottage, then keeping the hedge on your left join an access drive to the road.

Turn left, then right through Gonalston and just past a right hand bend take ιe path left into a field, aiming for the Church. After 150 metres you have the ιoice of either walking to the church, or turning right through a gate to meet the 612. Cross over to a gate and follow the bank on your left to emerge onto a road. ιrn left, go over Gonalston crossing and after 250 metres turn right alongside a ιream, which you follow swinging left at the end of the field, then right to join a ιidleway. Pass through a gate then turn right to Mill Farm.

Cross the bridge over the Dover Beck, pass through a gate and turn right over stile. Continue ahead then bear right to follow a bank right, to cross the railway ιe then continue still with the Beck right to a stile by the side of the A612. Cross ιer the stile and road to the minor road opposite and Cliff Mill.

Continue for 250 metres and the road bends right. Take the stile left. Over this, ιrn right, firstly following the Beck then veering left to aim for Lowdham Church, ιen in the distance. In the fourth field a hedge comes in from the right, keep to the ιft of it and forward into Lowdham village.

On reaching Main Street, turn left then right on a metalled path beside a ιhool. Cross the dual carriageway to the footpath opposite which leads back to ιe Church.

POINTS OF INTEREST

ιowdham:

ιhe church of St. Mary the Virgin was founded c1170, and has a Norman font and ιwer. Inside is the stone effigy of Sir Jon de Ludham, whose son accompanied ιdward III to the Battle of Crecy. The village school adopted this family's armorial ιearings as its badge.

ιear the church is the **Old Hall**, which is Elizabethan in parts, formerly called ιroughton Hall. In the grounds is a mound which was formerly a defensive ιrtification.Lowdham was surrounded by at least 10 corn mills:

ιowdham Mill is one of the most picturesque old mills in the county, having been ιstefully restored yet still retaining traces of its life as a working mill.

ιowdham Grange was the home of Charles Storer. In 1930 it became the first open' ιorstal, but closed in recent years. However, it is to be re-opened as a prison.

Gonalston:

The church of St. Lawrence was rebuilt in 1853 and contains three monuments t the Heriz family dating from c1300: two knights and Lady Mathilda.

Look out for the old **Smithy** in **Gonalston** with its horseshoe-shaped entrance an datestone of 1854. This is well worth a photograph.

Hoveringham Mill, nowadays a private dwelling, has again been restore although only the mill race remains to remind us of its former purpose.

Cliff Mill was previously used to produce textiles using child labour gathere from London orphanages. It has now been converted to residential apartments.

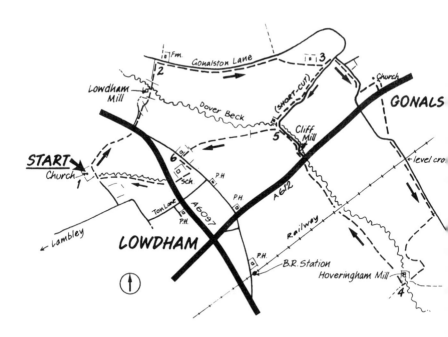

WALK 40

41. Smug and Silver Trent

A circular walk taking in the River Trent, Gedling village and Burton Joyce with excellent views along the Trent Valley, with a shorter ramble following the River Trent at Stoke Bardolph.

THE FACTS

Area:	Burton Joyce, Stoke Bardolph, Gedling, Lambley	
Distance:	Long walk:	14 km (8.5 miles)
	Short walk:	8.5 km (5 miles)
Duration:	Long walk:	4 hours
	Short walk:	2.5 hours

Maps Required: OS Pathfinder 833 (SK 43/53) Nottingham (South West),

834 (SK 63/73) Radcliffe on Trent & Keyworth and

813 (SK 64/74) Carlton & Elston

OS Landranger 129 Nottingham & Loughborough

Bus/Train Link: Nottingham

Terrain: Riverside paths and field tracks, moderate climbing, good views

Starting Point: Riverside Car Park, Stoke Lane near Burton Joyce Railway Station SK 646430

Refreshments: Ferry Boat Inn, Stoke Bardolph; Shops and Public Houses in Burton Joyce and Lambley

THE ROUTE

1. From the car park walk upstream towards Stoke Bardolph following the

135

WALK 41

riverside path to reach the Ferry Boat Inn. Continue along the riverside path walking past Stoke Lock and continue until just before the railway viaduct.

2.   Just before the viaduct, turn right, keeping the raised banking of the slurry lagoons on your right and the floodlit installation of the rail oil terminal on your left for a distance of about 1 km. At the end of the raised banking, turn right and head towards the Ouse Beck, where you will find a footbridge. *It should be noted that plans are in hand to drain the lagoons in the near future and return them to agricultural land - much to the disappointment of local naturalists who recognise its importance as a roosting place for migratory birds.*

2a. **Short route variation:** Instead of turning left our path goes straight across fields aiming for the Stoke Bardolph sewage works seen in the distance. Keep a straight line aiming for a left field edge path to reach Stoke Lane. Cross the road and take the footpath opposite to reach a bend in the track. Turn left along the track to reach a watercourse. Turn right and take the path parallel to the watercourse to reach Stoke Lane with the Ferry Boat Inn on the right. To return to the car park, turn left and retrace the road back.

3.   Turn left and follow the path to a trading estate. At the end of the ditch, follow the hedge to the right for 50 metres, then follow the path to the right by a stile, keeping the hedge on the left. Go past a gate and continue to the road. Turn left and go under a bridge. Take the footpath to the right over a rail bridge, then turn left across the recreation ground, aiming for the traffic lights seen on the far left corner. Cross the road, and turn left to walk up Brooklands Drive. Take the twitchell at the first bend to reach Waverley Avenue, continuing ahead to reach Main Road, Gedling.

4.   Cross using the pelican crossing, turn left and then take the path uphill through All Hallows church. Rejoin the road to turn right into Jessops Lane.

5.   Continue along Jessops Lane to reach a small, grassed area on the right leading into the recreation ground. Cross the bridge on the left and walk to the far right corner. Turn left to pass under a railway bridge to reach Yew Tree Lane. Continue along Yew Tree Lane to take the footpath near the end of the road across school grounds. Turn left at the end going between hedges. Cross the road and take the footpath to continue straight up the road to reach Almond Walk.

6.   Take the footpath to the left to reach fields. Continue uphill crossing several fields with stiles passing west of Gedling Wood to reach Spring Lane, Lambley.

7.   Take the bridleway to the right past Wood Farm and follow the bridlepath to a gate. Turn right past Stockhill Farm then turn left to follow a path through a further gate to pass a wind pump, where we turn right along a further bridleway.

8.   Follow this bridle road downhill to join Lambley Lane. Keep walking downhill to reach Main Street and cross to Church Road A612. **Cross over with care** and walk down St. Helen's Crescent. At the end go under a subway under the railway to reach the River Trent. Turn right and walk along the riverside path back to the car park and the end of the walk.

POINTS OF INTEREST

Burton Joyce:

A recent landowner in this village was the 5th Earl of Caernarvon, who became famous on his discovery of the tomb of Tutankhamen. Old buildings of interest in the village include the manor house and examples of framework knitters' cottages. The church of St. Helen's dates in part from Medieval times.

Ferry Boat Inn, Stoke Bardolph - there used to be a ferry across the Trent at this point to Shelford.

Gedling:

When William Peveril built Nottingham Castle, he was given 10 acres of land to make an orchard at Gedling, which survived into living memory just below the church on Grimm Lane (now Jessops Lane).

All Hallows Church has a remarkable steeple, all of which dates from the 14th century.

Lambley:

This was originally an agricultural community which then expanded in the 19th century as a centre for framework knitting. By 1844 there were 381 stocking frames in the village.

Holy Trinity Church was built in the will of Ralph Cromwell, Lord Treasurer of England in the late 14th century.

42. The Byron Walk

The walk starts from the Parish Church of St. Mary Magdalene in Hucknall Market Place. Lord Byron is buried in the family vaults by the choir stalls in this church. We also visit the Byron family tombs at Newstead Abbey and Papplewick Church which is associated with the Robin Hood legend.

THE FACTS

Area:	Hucknall, Linby, Newstead Abbey
Distance:	12.5 km (7.75 miles)
Duration:	3.75 hours
Maps Required:	OS Pathfinder 795 (SK 45/55) Sutton in Ashfield and 812 (SK 44/54) Nottingham North
	OS Landranger 120 Mansfield & Worksop and 129 Nottingham & Loughborough
Bus/Train Link:	Hucknall
Terrain:	Mainly surfaced tracks, easy walking. Entrance fee payable to go through Newstead Abbey grounds.
Starting Point:	Hucknall Market Place SK 534494 Parking in Market Place except Thursdays and Fridays (Market days). Alternative parking on South Street, just off the Market Place: please check current restrictions and obtain necessary tickets.
Refreshments:	Hucknall: several places; Newstead Abbey; Linby

THE ROUTE

1. Turn left out of the church gates and cross the market place to the old Co-Operative building where a statue of Lord Byron can be found recessed in the wall

139

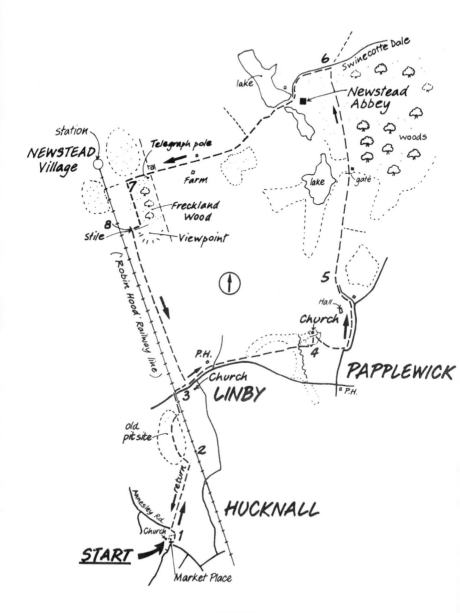

WALK 42

at first floor level. Pass to the right of the building following the main road round a left-hand bend before immediately crossing over and turning right down Carlingford Road.

2.	Carlingford Road is a no-through road to vehicles, but at the end continue ahead by bearing immediately left and right on to Linby Walk. After 150 metres turn left over a stile towards a grassed hill on the former Linby Colliery site. After 100 metres branch left along the path over the summit. At a junction of the paths with the church in view to the right, turn right and follow the path down to a gate.

3.	Turn left and in a short distance join the main road. Turn right and carry straight on over the level crossing and a roundabout to pass through Linby village, passing the two village crosses and public house, and continuing along the road for a further 800 metres where the road bends to the right, turn left through a gate to walk a footpath along the left edge of a field.

4.	After passing through a small copse the path ascends gently. Half way up the rise turn left through a gap in the hedge to follow a short path to Papplewick Church. Leave the church by the main drive and keep straight on ahead to the main road. Turn left and walk along the pavement for about 400 metres to where the road bends to the right, passing Papplewick Hall.

5.	Turn left at the footpath sign on to a broad track. After a short distance follow a bend to the right then continue straight ahead for just over a kilometre to the iron gate entrance to Newstead Abbey Estate. Pass through the gates into the grounds of Newstead Abbey and keep straight ahead for a further kilometre in the same direction. Newstead Abbey itself is visible to the left.

6.	Eventually you will meet the main metalled drive to the Abbey. Turn left and follow this to the main Abbey building which is famous for being the ancestral home of the Byron family.

Note: when turning left onto the metalled drive you are leaving the public right of way through the Abbey Grounds and **you must pay** the entrance fee to enter. The Abbey and water gardens are well worth taking the time to explore.

After visiting the Abbey, keep on in the same direction along the metalled drive through the Abbey Estate. Continue along the road for 2 kilometres to pass through two Lodge gates, the last one having a pay kiosk, before going out of the Abbey grounds.

7.   Turn left immediately. You now have two choices: *either to take the surfaced path past the electricity pole to join directly the former railway track,* **or** to go over the stile into the former pit tip, now created as Freckland Wood, part of the Greenwood Forest Initiative. **Remember to keep to the track - do not walk through the planted tree areas.** Walk up the hill to the top of the ridge. Stop and enjoy the splendid view. Then continue along the ridge path to take the first right to drop down to a stile.

8.   Turn left, joining the level route along the disused railway line, which has been resurfaced for the use of walkers and cyclists. Follow this track until it comes out on the outskirts of Linby near the level crossing encountered earlier in the walk. Retrace your steps by turning right over the level crossing and then left onto the path. However, on this occasion do not ascend the hill, but keep left along the path which skirts the bottom of the disused colliery site. Follow this path until it joins Carlingford Road then retrace your steps back to the Market Place.

POINTS OF INTEREST

Hucknall:

The poet George Gordon Byron is buried in the Byron family vault of the church of St. Mary Magdalen, which stands in the Market Square. Byron's memorial inside is a simple tablet with a profile medallion above. The church also has a fine example of late Victorian stained glass.

Linby:

The Medieval church of St. Michael has in the churchyard 163 unmarked graves of pauper children who were brought from London during the Industrial Revolution to work in textile mills along the river Leen. They were victims of the harsh mill conditions and smallpox.

The village has a stream running the length of the main street to join the river Leen, and has two stone crosses and a maypole. The top cross has a rare seven-sided base and was renovated in 1869 after being damaged by the Puritans in the 1650s. The bottom cross was erected c1660 to celebrate the Restoration of the monarchy, and had the stream running under its base.

The village has several 18th century framework knitters' cottages, and was the scene of serious Luddite riots in 1812.

142

Newstead Abbey:

This was founded in c1165 by Henry II as a Priory for Augustinian Canons. After the Dissolution of the monasteries it became a country house, which was owned by the Byron family from 1540, and now contains many relics of the Byron family.

At the Dissolution the monks threw the brass lectern into one of the lakes, which was dredged some 200 years later and found to contain documents in the pedestal. The lake is still called Eagle Pond. Nearby is a marble monument to Boatswain - Byron's dog.

At the Abbey gates stands the Pilgrim Oak, an ancient tree said to have been planted before the Dissolution in 1539 at a site traditionally used by rustic people to celebrate festivals.

The poet, the sixth Lord Byron inherited the estate from his great uncle at the age of 10. The estate had then been ruined, and the Abbey mortgaged and was completely uninhabitable. In his youth the poet was educated at Harrow and Cambridge, but came back to Newstead for holidays, and he eventually moved here when he was 21. His extravagant lifestyle led to mounting debts, and in 1817 he was forced to sell the estate.

Papplewick:

The church of St. James has a 14th century tower and inside is a musicians' gallery and the village squire's pew with its own fireplace.

In the churchyard is a memorial stone to Oliver Measley, a former steward of Newstead Abbey with whom Lord Byron stayed in 1803. (The stone is well hidden!) Several other Abbey servants were also buried here.

Along a footpath leading into Newstead Abbey grounds it is possible, with the owner's permission, to see what is known as Robin Hood's Stable: a cave where it is said Robin Hood kept his horses.

Just outside the village is the Victorian Papplewick Pumping Station, now restored and running at steam at advertised times.

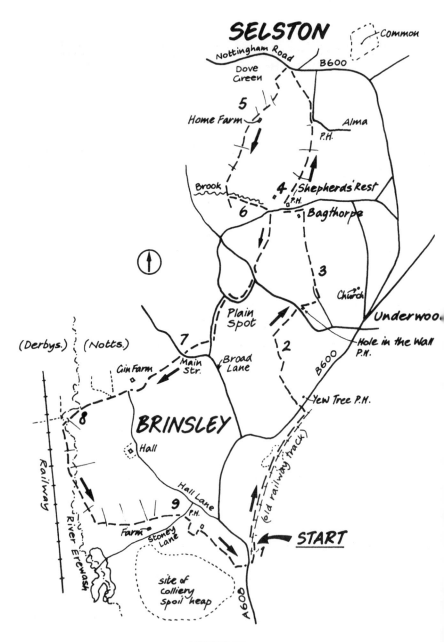

WALK 43

43. Pit Ponies and Shepherds!

A walk full of surprises, all of them pleasant, in an area where mining is fast becoming a memory. Most of the footpaths here are over grass, a contrast with the arable east of the county.

THE FACTS

Area:	Brinsley, Underwood, Bagthorpe, Selston
Distance:	13 km (8 miles)
Duration:	4 hours
Maps Required:	OS Pathfinder 812 (SK 44/54) Nottingham (North) and 795 (SK 45/55) Sutton in Ashfield
	OS Landranger 129 Nottingham and Loughborough and 120 Mansfield and Worksop
Bus/Train Link:	Eastwood
Terrain:	A few not too steep climbs
Starting Point:	Car Park on A608 south of Brinsley SK 464485
Refreshments:	Robin Hood, White Lion and Yew Tree, Brinsley; Shepherd's Rest, Bagthorpe; Hole in the Wall, Underwood

THE ROUTE

1. Next to the car park is an old mineral railway: follow this north through pleasant woodland until a path veers left to Cordy Lane opposite the Yew Tree public house. Turn right, then left into a twitchell beside a postbox. Follow the edge of pasture, then another twitchell to a lane. Walk up the hill about 100 metres and cross the stile left.

2. Keep uphill in grass fields, turning right along the top side of the former pit

145

heap. Cross two stiles and follow the tarmac path ahead to twin kissing-gates, the continue to the Hole in the Wall public house at Underwood. Opposite the public house is a little path leading to a terraced street, where you turn left.

3.   At the bottom of the street cross the stile, go down the hill to a gate, continue to the left-hand corner of the next field and down, still on grassland, to enter the yard of Brookside Farm. Pass the farm and keep right to a road. Turn left through the tiny hamlet of Bagthorpe as far as the Shepherd's Rest public house. *At this point the walk can be shortened by two miles by continuing to a stile on the left, and continue at paragraph 6.*

4.   After the pub, turn right, pass left of the pub and keep straight ahead on a well-trodden path. At a road go ahead as far as a fenced path on the left. Follow this to a street, cross it and go up the unsurfaced road to join the B600 in Selston. Turn left, then first left again into Lea Lane: ignore the first avenue left, but take the second which leads down to Home Farm.

5.   The path passes right of the farm to a gap beside a farm gate, continues downhill beside the hedge and crosses a footbridge. Angle slightly right in the first grass field, keep left in the next and cross the Bagthorpe Brook and the stile just beyond it. Turn left here and follow the brook and left-hand hedge, cross a stile and go on to the road in Bagthorpe. The Shepherd's Rest is just to your left.

6.   Cross the road to a stile and follow the hedge uphill, then keep to the left of two more pasture fields. *Crich Stand is visible from this point.* Turn left up a road and right along Plainspot Road. Follow this road in a left turn and look out for the Primitive Methodist church (now unfrocked) on the right near the foot of the hill. Turn right along the back lane and continue in a meadow to another road.

7.   Cross straight over and take the right-hand path down to a stream, across a causeway and left down a field edge. Continue across the next field and ahead to a fenced path by-passing Gin Farm. Go downhill on the middle road, which continues as a green lane. A wide grass path leads to a bridge over the River Erewash, which you cross for a brief visit into Derbyshire.

8.   Go forward 50 metres and turn left to a double stile, then go forward to another. Angle slightly left to cross another bridge and follow the clear path, ignoring a stile on your left. Keep ahead to a stile, then to another and turn left up the field to the corner. In the next field aim slightly right to a stile and follow a clear uphill path to join Stoney Lane.

9.   If suffering from thirst, turn left up the lane, then right to the White Lion or Robin Hood public houses, and continue to your starting point. To use a new bridleway cross Stoney Lane, go on to a path junction where you turn right, following the right-hand hedge to a stile at the top and then follow the bridleway left to your starting point.

POINTS OF INTEREST

Brinsley:

In the 12th century, the Duke of Devonshire built the Hall and Manor House, both of which still survive as farms. Pollington colliery closed in 1919 and Bodtod colliery some time later. Before its headstocks were removed, it was used in the filming of D.H. Lawrence's *Sons and Lovers*, in which many Brinsley residents were used as extras.

The church was originally called St. Saviour's but the name was later changed to St. James. The village did have 10 public houses at one time, but only 5 now remain, the oldest being the Robin Hood coach house.

Underwood and Bagthorpe:

Both villages are part of the parish of Selston. Underwood was a former colliery village, with rows of terraced houses. The headstocks now stand in the churchyard of St. Michael and All Saints.

Selston:

St. Helen's church has a Norman font with a mobile history. 200 years ago it was removed from the church and taken to Blackwell. It was then returned, not to the church, but to the Bull & Butcher Inn, where it was fixed to the pump. Later it was used as a flower pot in a private garden, to be rescued in 1906 by Rev. Charles Harrison who restored it to its proper place.

The churchyard houses the grave of Dan Boswell, king of the gypsies. For many years the gypsies would return to Selston to pay their respects, and their new-born babies were brought to the church to be baptised. Dan's epitaph reads:

"I've lodged in many a town,
I've travelled many a year,
But death at length has brought me down
To my last lodging here."

44. Greasley Circular

A surprisingly rural ramble from Greasley Church through beautiful woodlands and experiencing one of the best ridgeway paths in the county, as well as seeing the remains of Beauvale Priory, Moorgreen Reservoir and Greasley Castle.

THE FACTS

Area:	Moorgreen, Greasley
Distance:	8 km (5 miles) plus an optional extension to Felley Hill
Duration:	2.5 hours (optional extension: 3.5 hours)
Maps Required:	OS Pathfinder 812 (SK 44/54) Nottingham (North) & Ilkeston
	OS Landranger 120 Mansfield & Worksop and 129 Nottingham & Loughborough
Bus/Train Link:	Eastwood
Terrain:	Easy with a few inclines, but may be muddy in wet weather
Starting Point:	Lay-by on B600 outside Greasley Church SK 490472
Refreshments:	Minton Cafe, Greasley Church; Horse & Groom, Moorgreen

THE ROUTE

1.   From the lay-by walk along the roadside towards Nottingham as far as Greasley Castle Farm. Cross the road at its entrance and go over stile opposite.

2.   Follow the field edge path and climb up the hill, over a second stile and up to the top corner (signpost). *Excellent views from this point. This part of the walk passes a memorial bench erected by the Broxtowe Ramblers in memory of Lew Pykett.*

3.   Turn right and walk along a field edge path, going into another field as it bends left, then walk to the corner of this field, turn right again and walk down to a further signpost.

4.   Turn left and through a gap in the hedge, keep a straight line beside the hedge until reaching a small bridge.

5.   Cross over bridge and walk towards the right-hand corner of the field ahead where there is a bridge crossing the Giltbrook.

6.   Cross the bridge, turn left and follow the edge of the field to reach a gap in part of the fence ahead. On the left is the source of the Giltbrook. Keep straight on through the gap in the hedge, then turn sharp right and walk to the corner of the field.

7.   Over the stile, turn left onto New Road and continue along the road to reach the edge of the wood with a finger post directing you to Hucknall, Annesley and Underwood.

Before doing this, however, take the opportunity of looking at the site of Beauvale Priory. Walk a further 120 metres to the bend in the road seen ahead. *Look over the right-hand hedge to see the remains of Beauvale Priory with a farmhouse and buildings. The remains are on private land.* Return to the footpath sign.

8.   Climb over the stile and follow a wide track at the side of a plantation. Continue beyond the wood to a field hedge at the side of the M1 motorway. At the 3-way wooden finger post, turn left and follow the track to enter the wood. Follow the woodland path seen ahead until it reaches a stone surface path.

9.   Turn right at this point and follow the track, which soon turns left, continue to climb uphill to a junction where five paths meet.

10. Walk straight on, following a narrow forest track to reach the wood edge. *The view of Felley Priory from this point is impressive: savour it for a few minutes.*

11. **Longer route extension:** Turn right and follow the track alongside the wood edge to a path under the M1 motorway. On the other side of the motorway, turn left and climb the hill to follow the track which eventually passes cottages on the right to arrive at a T-junction.

At the junction, turn left, crossing the motorway again, then passing America Farm on the left. Continue along the track down to Felley Hill to another T-junction. At this junction turn left and then join up with the shorter route at paragraph 12.

11a. **Shorter alternative:** Turn left, following a wide track beside Morning Springs

Wood. After about 800 metres, where the track turns right across the field, our path continues along the edge of the wood as far as a row of oak trees. Follow the path on the right of the oaks and cross the grass bearing left to a stile by a fence.

12. Turn left and follow the well-surfaced bridleway going into High Park Wood. (There is a lower path by the water for part of this route. This rejoins the bridleway.) Continue along this for nearly 1.5 km, where it joins a metalled road. Continue along this to reach the B600 at Beauvale Lodge. *(To view the reservoir, turn right for 50 metres.)*

13. Pass through the gateway and turn left along the main road. Follow this through the outskirts of Moorgreen to reach the Horse and Groom public house.

14. Cross the road **with care** (signposted to Eastwood) and follow this right-hand fork until you reach a finger post on the left-hand side in 200 metres.

15. Follow the footpath to Greasley Church through a farmyard, over a stile and crossing a field to enter the graveyard of Greasley Church.

16. Walk to the Church, visit several interesting graves, including that of Benjamin Drawwater (Captain Cook's surgeon) and look over the wall to observe the remains of Greasley Castle. Return to the lay-by at the church gate entrance.

POINTS OF INTEREST

Greasley Castle Farm was originally the site of fortified manor house belonging to the Cantelupe family. They commenced building their first house on the site in c1341. Some of the moat and stone walling survive, and a ruined wall and reconstructed pointed arch were incorporated in the existing farm building, which dates from around 18th century.

Beauvale Priory was one of only nine Carthusian monasteries in England, and is the second best preserved, having been dissolved in 1539 after Robert Lawrence, the Prior, was imprisoned for refusing to acknowledge Henry VIII as Head of the Church of England. He and the ex-prior became the **Beauvale Martyrs** when they were executed as traitors in 1535. They are commemorated in an annual service held on the site of the monastic church. Note the large wall and traces of a fine church window.

The village of *Greasley* appeared in the Domesday Book.

St Mary's Church, Greasley The stained glass include two roundel windows taken from Beauvale Priory. There is an information board in the churchyard detailing several gravestones of interest.

Moorgreen Reservoir: this was built originally to feed the Nottingham Canal.

Beauvale House: built in the 19th century by Earl Cowper. The tall turreted tower on one side was apparently built at the insistence of his wife, who wanted to survey her domains.

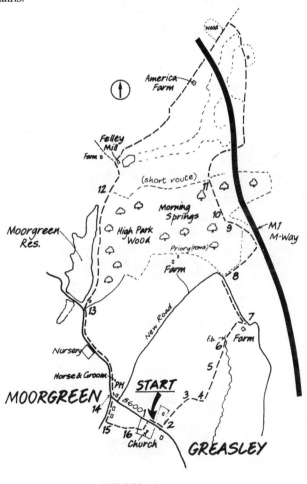

WALK 44

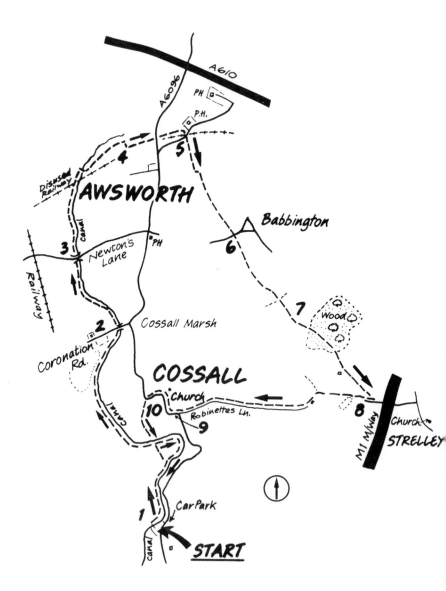

WALK 45

45. Erewash Ramble

Explore the Erewash Valley, the beautiful village of Cossall with its Lawrence connections and Awsworth, home of one of Nottinghamshire's dry ski slopes. A pleasant section of Nottingham Canal brings you back to your start.

THE FACTS

Area:	Cossall, Awsworth
Distance:	14 km (9 miles) plus 2 km (1 mile) extension to the Broad Oak public house
Duration:	4.5 hours (optional extension: 5 hours)
Maps Required:	OS Pathfinder 812 (SK 44/54) Nottingham North
	OS Landranger 129 Nottingham & Loughborough
Bus/Train Link:	Nottingham
Terrain:	Towpaths and field paths
Starting Point:	Field House Corner car park, Nottingham Canal SK 484412
Refreshments:	Broad Oak, Strelley; Hoggs Head, Awsworth

THE ROUTE

1.   Leave the car park by the gate, turn right and walk along the canal towpath for 1.4 km passing Stoney Lane to arrive at Coronation Road.

2.   Drop down off the towpath, cross Coronation Road and take the steps opposite to return to the canal towpath. Continue along the towpath to Newtons Lane.

3.   Cross Newtons Lane and regain the towpath with Bennerley Viaduct seen spanning the valley on your left. Continue to the end of the canal. At this point we

153

describe two routes: (a) the present route and *(b) the route when the Awsworth By-pass is built.*

a) Follow the path to the right going past Napha House and taking the footpath on the left before the railway bridge, climbing up the bank into a wood. Keep to the left side of the wood to emerge into a field, keeping the hedge on your right. Cross the Shilo Recreation Ground diagonally and exit with the old Station House on your right.

b) At the end of the canal, turn right, cross the Awsworth By-pass with care by the pedestrian refuge and turn left to take the track that goes up the bank onto a former railway line. Follow this until you reach the old Station House. Turn left off the railway line to join the road and footpath at 3a.

4.   Walk up the road parallel with the railway line seen on the right, and walk to Awsworth Main Street. Cross the road and take the path opposite. Cross the field and aim for the house opposite. Go through the stile past May Cottage to enter a small industrial estate. Follow this to the Gate Inn.

5.   Turn right along Main Street for 50 metres to take the footpath on the opposite side of the road. This path goes through a garden then over a stile to enter a large field. Follow the path straight on with the hedge on the left to reach a track. Turn left then immediately turn right, and follow the footpath with the hedge on the right over three fields to reach Westby Lane at Babbington village.

6.   Cross the road and take the path opposite to follow a well-marked track across a large field, through a small coppice then across three other fields to reach Strelley Park Farm which will be on your right.

7.   Cross the track, follow the path opposite across two fields, through Spring Wood, then across a field and follow the path to the left of Turkey Fields Farm, skirting a small spinney seen ahead to reach a bridleway. At this point, a detour can be taken by going left into Strelley village *(well worth a visit, and also an opportunity to visit the Broad Oak public house and return to this point).*

8.   Turn right and follow the bridleway for 500 metres to reach a footpath on the left opposite a track to Turkey Fields Farm. Follow this down a narrow track and over a stile into a field. Walk across the first field and then diagonally right across the second field to reach Robinetts Lane. Turn left and walk into the outskirts of Cossall.

9.   We reach Cossall on narrow roads with no pavements. **Walk with care** in this area. Walk up to the church along the main road.

10.   Continue along the main street to the next bend, take the footpath on the left going through a horse paddock to reach the track - Mill Lane. Cross this and take the path opposite and drop down the field to the canal. Over the bridge, take the stile opposite, and walk across the field to the stile seen ahead. Turn right and return to the car park.

POINTS OF INTEREST

Cossall:

The parish church of St. Catherine has a Waterloo monument in the churchyard. Also worth a visit are Church Cottage, the Parish Hall and Willoughby Almshouse.

Awsworth:

The brick church of St. Peter was built in 1746 by the coalmine owner Richard Smedley of Risley, of which the chancel is preserved.

Strelley:

The chancel in the church of All Saints was endowed in 1356 by Samson de Strelley who died about 1390 and lies buried with his wife in a fine alabaster tomb chest.

Strelley Hall stands next to the church, and the Medieval walls survive. The village also has examples of late 18th century estate cottages.

46. The Hemlock Stone

A varied walk taking in the intriguing Hemlock Stone, Stapleford Hill, giving views of three counties, the Nottingham and Erewash Canals and the Bramcote Hills.

THE FACTS

Area:	Stapleford, Bramcote Hills, Erewash Canal	
Distance:	Short Route	5 km (3 miles)
	Long Route	10 km (6.25 miles)
Duration:	Short Route	2 hours
	Long Route	3 hours
Maps Required:	OS Pathfinder 833 (SK 43/53) Nottingham (South West) and 812 (SK 44/54) Nottingham North;	
	OS Landranger 129 (Nottingham & Loughborough)	
Bus/Train Link:	Nottingham	
Terrain:	Field paths, steep climb to the Hemlock Stone	
Starting Point:	Bramcote Hills Car Park, Corner of Coventry Lane (A6002) and Ilkeston Road (A6007). Grid ref. SK 499384	
Refreshments:	Jaguar public house, Hickings Lane, Stapleford;	
	Trowell Garden Centre; Festival Inn, Trowell;	
	Bramcote Manor Public House	

THE ROUTE

1. From the car park, pass through the small opening into Coventry Lane *(please*

ote this road is scheduled for upgrading). Cross the road and walk up the Lane to the ∍ntrance way onto the open space of the Hemlock Stone/Stapleford Hill. Take the ⸱ath climbing up the hill to the Hemlock Stone.

⸱. At the Stone you have a choice, either to walk up to the long point' of ⸱tapleford Hill, or to take the path around the hill. To walk to Stapleford Hill ⸱ummit follow the path to the rear of the Hemlock Stone, that climbs uphill ⸱hrough a wooded area. Retrace your steps back to the Stone, and then take the ⸱ignposted path on your right (approx 120° turn) leading around the edge of the ⸱ill.

⸱. Continue through the wood bearing left at each junction until you reach the meadow area. Continue through the field where you turn right into a second field. Turn left and follow field edge path towards the railway line to reach a stile.

⸱. Over the stile, turn left on the wide path at the foot of an embankment going ⸱hrough a copse. At a fork, bear right, climb uphill then follow the path turning ⸱ight then left towards houses, car park and fence. **Do not** go through the gate but ⸱urn right following the fence at first, then into a narrow twitchell. **Unprotected ⸱ailway line not far ahead, so keep children and dogs close to you.**

5. Cross railway line with **great care**, then over the stile bear left across the field ⸱o another stile and junction of paths. *If you are taking the short route, turn right and ⸱ollow instructions from Section 12.* If following the long route, turn left returning to ⸱his point later in the walk.

⸱. Follow perimeter fence of Trowell Garden Centre (refreshments available in ⸱he cafe). Passing the entrance to the Garden Centre, cross the road and follow the ⸱arked path to Swansea Bridge. You leave the Robin Hood Way at Swansea Bridge by dropping down to the towpath on the near side of the canal and then ⸱urning left towards Trowell.

⸱. At the end of the towpath go down some steps, under the M1 bridge, the ⸱climb up steps back onto the canal. Continue along the towpath going under a ⸱oad bridge (Nottingham Road, Trowell) and continue along a canal now filled in ⸱and landscaped as a Linear Path. Continue for 800 metres to reach the footpath on ⸱he left. Leave the canal path, descend steps and continue along track to reach ⸱toney Lane.

⸱8. Turn left along Stoney Lane and continue to reach Ilkeston Road near railway bridge. Turn right, walk over the railway bridge, cross the road with great care and take the footpath up the lane (The Forge). Walk to the end of The Forge to reach stile and field gate, then cross two further stiles.

9.   Enter a grass meadow then aim for the large factory with a tall chimney seen ahead. After walking so far across the meadow, a green bridge comes into view. Aim for this. Cross the bridge and walk along the track to the Erewash Canal. Turn left along the towpath for 500 metres to reach the Lock.

10.   Turn left and leave the canal, going over a railway bridge, then through gateway continuing along a marked path to a bridge. Then forward under the railway to reach Ilkeston Road, Trowell. Turn right over a pelican crossing. Drink and food are available at the Festival Inn and there is the opportunity to visit St Helen's Church.

11.   Walk up Nottingham Road to rejoin the Canal. Return along the footpath going under the M1 then up to Swansea Bridge. Leave the canal, return to Trowell Garden Centre and take the path around the Garden Centre to rejoin the short route. Continue along the towpath for 1.6km to reach Coventry Lane.

12.   Cross the road, take the path opposite going under the railway bridge and continue until you reach Moor Lane. Turn right along Moor Lane and leave the wood to follow a well-marked track with playing field on the right. On reaching the T-junction, rejoin the Robin Hood Way.

13.   Continue straight on for 50 metres, turn right and take the footpath. Follow the footpath towards the first stile (you can leave the path here to visit Bramcote Manor for food and refreshments). Over the stile, then immediately over a second stile on the left, still following the boundary of the sports field.

14.   Climb up the hill to enter a wood. You are now on the Bramcote Hills. Take a diagonal path to the right, still climbing, to reach a path junction after 70 metres. Bear right, and follow the boundary fence to a quarry on the right. Keep parallel to the fence and take a left turn signposted Bramcote Park Car Park and drop downhill to reach the end of the walk.

POINTS OF INTEREST

Stapleford:

The church of St. Helen's dates from the Middle Ages. In the churchyard is a Cross erected before the Norman Conquest, the most important of its date in Nottinghamshire.

There are a series of framework knitters' cottages in Nottingham Road, with the typical long top windows.

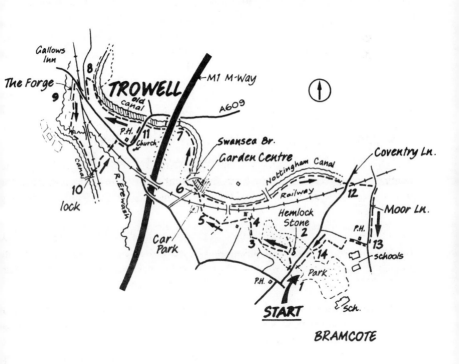

WALK 46

47. Medieval Churches and a Dovecote

Discover the three villages of Flintham, Syerston and Sibthorpe with their 13th century churches: a quiet corner of the county close to an ancient Roman road.

THE FACTS

Area:	Flintham, Syerston, Sibthorpe
Distance:	8 km (5 miles)
Duration:	2.5 hours
Maps Required:	OS Pathfinder 813 (SK 64/74) Carlton & Elston
	OS Landranger 129 Nottingham & Loughborough
Bus/Train Link:	Newark
Terrain:	Tracks, field paths and country roads
Starting Point:	Park by the old school and church, Flintham village SK 739461
Refreshments:	Boot & Shoe, Flintham

THE ROUTE

1.   From the church, walk along Inholms Road towards the new school for 300 metres. Turn right at the footpath sign and walk along the track to reach the sewage works. Turn right around the compound fence to a footbridge.

2.   Over the footbridge, continue ahead for 150 metres to a gap in the hedge. Pass through the hedge to the other field and continue along the field edge to reach Longhedge Lane. Turn right and then immediate left at the footpath sign. Cross the fields, aiming just right of Syerston Church, going over three stiles to reach the Main Street. Before reaching the road on entering a private garden, please respect their property.

3.   Turn right into the village and after 50 metres where the road forks, bear left to reach Low Farm after another 300 metres.

4.   Take the stile on the right to join a grassy track, reaching a green lane after 250 metres. Turn left for 1 km until reaching a farm bridge and footpath sign. Cross the large field in a south-easterly direction, aiming just left of Sibthorpe village seen ahead, to reach Dead Wong Lane. Turn right, and at the first junction right again (signed Flintham). *A short diversion would be to follow the footpath sign through Manor Farm yard turning right and first left to go to St. Peter's Church and see the Medieval dovecote. Retrace your steps to continue the walk.*

5.   Follow Flintham Road for almost 1 km to a sharp left bend. Turn right along Longhedge Lane (the course of an ancient road from the Trent to the Vale of Belvoir for 1.5 km.

6.   Just past a track from the right, take the field edge path to the left and continue for 900 metres to Butt Lane (Flintham). At the Main Street turn right to your start point.

POINTS OF INTEREST

Flintham:

Flintham Hall is a Medieval and Jacobean House, rebuilt in 1798, enlarged in 1829 and remodelled by T.C. Hine in 1853 for T.B.T. Hildyard MP. The Hall, Park and Gardens are open once a year.

Flintham Church of St. Augustine stands near the Hall and was rebuilt in 1828. Inside is a 14th century font with a 17th century cover and an effigy of c1330 knight bearing a shield.

Syerston:

Syerston Hall was built by the Fillingham family, agents of the Duke of Rutland. The Hall has a dovecote, coach house and garden house. The dovecote is believed to be over 700 years old and is over 20 metres in height, with 1,260 nesting places in 28 tiers.

The church of All Saints has little remaining from its 13th century origins.

Sibthorpe:

The church of St. Peter was built in the 13th century, with the chancel added in 1335 in connection with the foundation of a college of priests. Inside is an alabaster effigy to Edward Burnell who died in 1589.

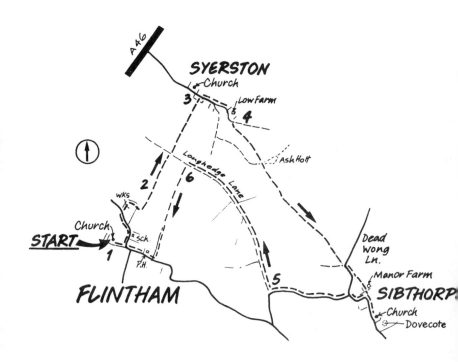

WALK 47

48. Windmill Walk

An easy walk high above the Trent Valley giving distant views of the City of Nottingham and a chance to see the remains of one of the last post' type windmills in the county.

THE FACTS

Area:	East Bridgford, Newton
Distance:	6 km (3.5 miles)
Duration:	1.75 hours
Maps Required:	OS Pathfinder 813 (SK 64/74) Carlton & Elston
Link:	OS Landranger 129 Nottingham & LoughboroughBus/Train Bingham
Terrain:	Field paths and a short section of minor road. The field paths can be muddy after rain.
Starting Point:	Village car park, Main Street, East Bridgford SK 694429
Refreshments:	The Royal Oak and The Reindeer, both East Bridgford

THE ROUTE

1.   From the car park turn left along Main Street and in 50 metres left into Walnut Tree Lane. Follow this for 250 metres to a crossroads, then turn right into Brunt's Lane which you follow to its junction with the A6097.

2.   Cross over to the gap opposite and forward across an arable field to reach a paddock after 500 metres and a stile right. Turn left over the stile, keeping in the same direction as previously, to cross two further stiles to emerge onto the main road through Newton village.

3.   Turn right for 1.2 km along the road, taking care for the last 600 metres as there

163

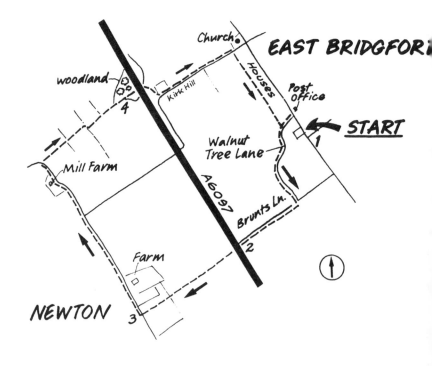

WALK 48

no footway. Just beyond Mill Farm where the road bends sharp left, turn right to follow the left hand edge of two fields, passing the ruined Newton Windmill on the right. At the end of the second field, climb a stile then follow the clear path turning right, then left, aiming for East Bridgford Mill to come back to the main road.

Cross over and just through the fence opposite turn right onto a metalled track and in 50 metres left onto a minor road into East Bridgford. After 300 metres take the footpath right through a paddock, passing the converted windmill left, to enter a narrow hedged path. Continue, passing between two houses into a field along a left field edge path. Then walk through a gate entering a hedge path, which leads into Walnut Tree Lane. Turn left to bring you back to Main Street, then right to the car park.

POINTS OF INTEREST

Only the brick base of *Newton Windmill*, built in the 19th century, now remains. It was unusual as it was a post mill, whereby the entire upper structure, usually of wood, rotates. This type of mill was not as durable as tower mills, which is why so few have survived. Another ruined one can be seen at Besthorpe, near Newark, whilst another at Kirk Hallam, near Ilkeston, Derbyshire, is in the process of restoration.

East Bridgford:

The local family of Hacker was involved in the Civil War, and Francis Hacker, a Parliamentarian, escorted Charles I to the scaffold, and was executed himself in 1660 after the Restoration.

St. Peter's Church is known to have been plundered by the Danes in the 9th century, while on their way up the River Trent. The church was rebuilt almost immediately.

Gypsum was mined in the village for over 200 years, until 1936.

East Bridgford Mill has now been converted to a private dwelling, but still retains much of its original structure. Despite the fact that the sails are long gone, the building still manages to dominate the surrounding houses.

49. In Robert Thoroton's Footsteps

Enjoy a pleasing walk through arable countryside and villages with a rustic charm.

THE FACTS

Area:	Hawksworth, Thoroton, Orston
Distance:	8 km (5 miles)
Duration:	2.5 hours
Maps Required:	OS Pathfinder 813 (SK 64/74) Carlton & Elston
	OS Landranger 120 Nottingham & Loughborough
Bus/Train Link:	Newark
Terrain:	Arable fields (well marked) tracks and some roadway.
Starting Point:	Hawksworth Church SK 753434
	Park along Main Street or Town Street
Refreshments:	Durham Ox public house, Orston

THE ROUTE

1.   From the main street go down the side of Hawksworth Church (Town Street) to the bottom (cul de sac) and turn right down a track. Pass through a gate and follow the path diagonally to the far corner of the field, to a gap in the hedge. Turn left along the road and at the top of the rise turn right at a footpath sign. Here is a large, open field. Follow the path in the general direction of a pylon in the far corner of the field. Halfway across, when you have just passed the line of Thoroton church spire on your left-hand side, turn in that direction on a line just to the right-hand side of the spire. Pass over a farm track to a stile. Cross over and go straight ahead to a gate. Pass through onto a road and turn right into Thoroton.

2.   Go along the road, passing a round, thatched dovecote on your left-hand side. About 100 metres past the dovecote, you reach a telegraph pole next to a farm. Turn left down the path, cross over a stile and follow the fence round. When the fence ends, bear right with the dyke on your right-hand side to another stile, with a footbridge over the River Smite. Cross over and turn right. Follow the river bank to the first hedge, turn left and after about 20 metres pass through the hedge. Turning left, follow the hedge to the corner of the field. Bearing right, with the hedge still on your left, go forward until the hedge ends at a corner. Just before this, turn left through the hedge onto a very long footbridge. Carry on forward with a fence on your right until you reach a way-marked open gateway. You are now on the edge of Orston. *(To reach the Durham Ox, you will have to walk down the lane and turn left at the main road.)*

3.   From here, with your back to the metalled road and Orston, follow the bridleway forward across several fields. The path is fairly well defined and each hedge is way-marked. On reaching the metalled road you turn left.

4.   Follow the road passing over the River Smite for the second time. On the other side about 60 metres on the left-hand side is a footbridge, with high sides. Go over, following a path across the field to the way-marked angle of an adjacent field. Go to the right-hand side and walk with the hedge on your left to a metalled road and turn right. About 60 metres before a crossroads, turn left through a gap in the hedge.

5.   Head straight across the field to the right of the wood in front of you. Enter the wood on the path bearing left and follow it through to the other side. Keep going forward across a field (there is a telegraph pole 25 metres to the right of your path). Cross over a concrete bridge onto a grassy track and keep on going to a metalled road. Turn left and walk into Hawksworth.

POINTS OF INTEREST

Hawksworth:

The church of St. Mary and All Saints has a brick tower. The Manor house is of stone, and has a stone dovecote dated 1665. The Manor Farm has a range of barns dated 1820.

Orston:

A drum from the Battle of Waterloo is kept in St. Mary's Church, which also has some Medieval wall paintings. The village was famous for gypsum workings since Medieval times, and once housed the most efficient plaster works in Europe until it went bankrupt in 1873. The site of what was the mill is just outside the village, and records show there had been a mill there since 1216. The last mill was dismantled in 1916 and shipped to New Zealand, where it became the first working windmill.

Thoroton: The church of St. Helen is a fine 13th century church, and in a farmyard there is a circular 14th century dovecote with a thatched roof.

The family of Dr. Robert Thoroton, the well-known Nottinghamshire historian, took their name from the village.

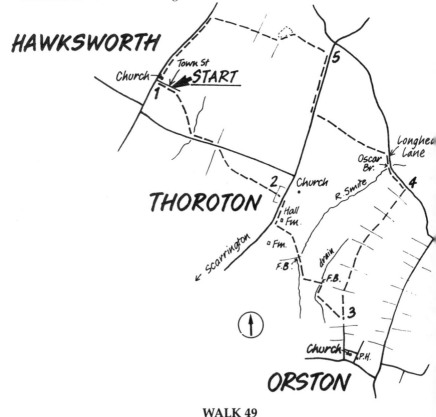

WALK 49

50. Archbishop Cranmer's Walk

An easy to follow walk linking three attractive villages on the edge of the Vale of Belvoir. A recently diverted footpath follows the River Smite between Aslockton and Orston.

THE FACTS

Area: Aslockton, Orston, Whatton

Distance: 8 km (5 miles)

Duration: 2.5 hours

Maps Required: OS Pathfinder 834 (SK 63/73) Radcliffe on Trent and 813 (SK 64/74) Carlton & Elston

OS Landranger 129 Nottingham & Loughborough

Bus/Train Link: Nottingham

Terrain: Level and fairly dry

Starting Point: Aslockton Church SK 743402

Refreshments: Durham Ox, Orston; Griffin's Head, Whatton; Old Greyhound and Cranmer Arms, Aslockton

THE ROUTE

1. Facing Aslockton Church, go through the farm gate just to the right of the churchyard and follow the farm track, keeping left around farm buildings. *On the left are traces of a motte and bailey castle, known as "Cranmer's Mound", though the future Archbishop, who was born in Aslockton, lived here long after the castle was abandoned.* The track leads into a grass field where the humps and bumps of the castle bailey can be seen: ignore the farm gate and keep to the left, following a low bank to the corner where there are a stile and a plank bridge. Continuing in the same direction, follow the edge of the next field, pass through a gap right as way-marked and go ahead to the River Smite.

2. The path, which used to cut across the middle of several fields, has recently

been diverted to the riverside with the agreement of walking groups and the farmers concerned. Being now at the field edge, the path should never be ploughed. Turning to your left, follow the pleasant path by the river for over a mile, passing "The Gallops" where race horses are exercised. Especially pleasant are the last three fields, which are grass. Trees shade the river, mostly ash and sycamore, and a few hawthorns have been allowed to grow.

3.　　On joining a road near Orston, turn right to pass through an avenue of mature horse chestnuts with a scattering of oak and ash. Continuing into the village, enter Chapel Street on the right. *At this point the Durham Ox could be visited in Church Street opposite.*

4.　　Go down Chapel Street, pass the chapel itself and continue to cross the footbridge at the end of the lane. Turn left along a hedged path which winds between gardens and tiny paddocks to emerge on Lombard Street. The high-hedged Moor Lane on the right is your route to Whatton, narrowing after half a mile as it passes old clay pits. Continue along a track at the left-hand side of a field, pass under the Nottingham to Grantham railway and keep on to reach a bridge over the dyke on your right. With Whatton Church in the distance, aim left and for the far end of a woodland strip, again on your left. Turn left over a concrete bridge following the way-marked route to join the long, green Orston Lane which brings you to Whatton, with the village green before you and the Griffin's Head to your left.

5.　　Turning right for a few metres, then right again into Main Street, make your way to Whatton Church by taking the left fork at two junctions. After passing the church turn left along a tiny lane to reach a handgate. An interesting collection of scrap iron is attached to ensure that it closes behind you! Cross the River Smite just beyond the gate. A delightful path follows the edges of two pastures, then crosses the railway and winds between houses to Aslockton's Main Street.

Emerging opposite the Old Greyhound, you have only to turn right past Cranmer's Cottage and the Cranmer Arms to return to the church.

POINTS OF INTEREST

Aslockton:

This was the birthplace of Archbishop Cranmer in 1489. He spent his childhood here, before going to Cambridge University at the age of 14. Only the ancient motte, known as *Cranmer's Mound* remains to recall the manor house which was situated near by.

Orston:

The River Smite flows through the village, which is home to an 18th century hall. A drum from the Battle of Waterloo is kept in St. Mary's Church, which also has some Medieval wall paintings. The village was famous for gypsum workings since Medieval times, and once housed the most efficient plaster works in Europe until it went bankrupt in 1873. The site of what was the mill is just outside the village, and records show there had been a mill there since 1216. The last mill was dismantled in 1916 and shipped to New Zealand, where it became the first working windmill.

Whatton:

The church of St. John of Beverley has connections with the Cranmer family, with a tomb chest of Thomas Cranmer who died in 1501, the father of the Archbishop, whilst the impressive Georgian manor stands in close proximity.

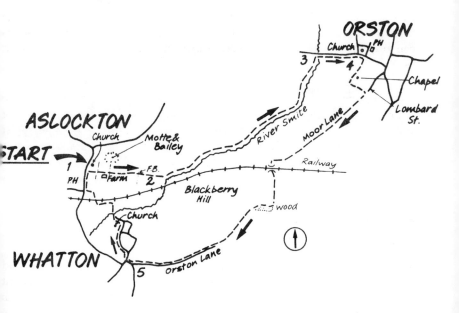

WALK 50

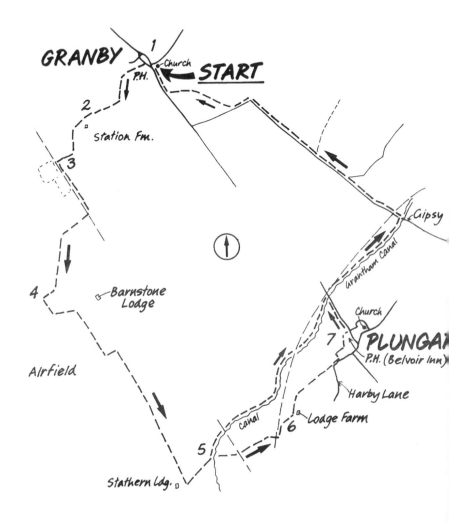

GRANBY

1

Church

P.H.

START

2

Station Fm.

3

Gipsy

Grantham Canal

4

Barnstone Lodge

Church

7

PLUNGAR

P.H. (Belvoir Inn)

Airfield

Harby Lane

canal

6

Lodge Farm

5

Stathern Ldg.

WALK 51

51. The Nobles of Belvoir (The Dukes of Rutland & Marquis of Granby)

Through the Vale of Belvoir runs the Grantham Canal, disused but attractive to nature lovers and walkers alike. An easy walk between two quiet villages in this broad vale links the counties of Nottinghamshire and Leicestershire and follows field paths, farm tracks and a stretch of the canal towpath.

THE FACTS

Area:	Granby, Plungar, Barkston le Vale
Distance:	14 km (8.5 miles)
Duration:	4.5 hours
Maps Required:	OS Pathfinder 834 (SK 63/73) Radcliffe on Trent
	OS Landranger 129 Nottingham & Loughborough
Bus/Train Link:	Nottingham
Terrain:	Vale of Belvoir is wide and shallow, so no climbs: can get muddy underfoot after rain.
Starting Point:	Granby Church SK 751362
Refreshments:	Marquis of Granby and Boot & Shoe, Granby; Belvoir Inn, Plungar

THE ROUTE

1. Start near Granby Church and set off along Church Street past a small triangular green and the "Old Post House", taking note of the Marquis of Granby' and Boot and Shoe' for future reference. Follow the street right, then enter a short lane on your left to a stile 30 metres right of the corner of the field. On the ridge away to your left stands Belvoir Castle, home of the Duke of Rutland. Cross the

next field, keeping slightly to the right of the stream, to another stile, then veer left to follow the stream and cross the new bridge just beyond Station Farm.

2.   Aim half-right to the corner of the field: if there is no stile there is a gate nearby. Go along the narrow meadow to another gate just before the far right-hand corner. A short track leads to a disused railway, one of many reminders in the Vale of its past importance as a source of iron.

3.   Turn left to follow it past another source of mineral wealth, a disused quarry. Thirty metres before reaching a barrier across the track turn right down a bank and across a footbridge. Continue beside the perimeter fence of the quarry along a path which can get overgrown in summer but is usually easily walkable, then after crossing a footbridge head half-left to the corner of the meadow.

4.   Here you join a good track which you follow to the left. After turning the corner by a cottage, don't go ahead to Barnstone Lodge after 100 metres, but follow the cement lane to the right and keep to the way-marked bridleway along the edge of Langar airfield. This is largely given over to industry, but crops grow between runways and perimeter track.

Just before the end of the hedge on your right, turn sharp left to walk between a wire fence and a tall hedge, then turn right over a footbridge and follow the edge of an arable field. At the end of this, swing right to rejoin the perimeter of the airfield. Turn left to follow it and go straight ahead along a farm track to Stathern Lodge. At the former farm, turn left past Canal Cottage to a substantial bridge before angling left to a gap in the opposite hedge, beyond which is the Grantham Canal.

5.   Two alternatives are available at this point: *the easier is to follow the canal towpath left for about 2.4 km, with perhaps a diversion to Plungar at the next road,* but the excellent field-path route needs some explanation.

Cross the canal and after a gate head straight ahead, converging with the far hedge. Soon after joining it, a bridge takes you over the disused railway you met before. After crossing it, keep beside the right-hand hedge to a stile and go forward to a bridge which crosses another railway track. After the second bridge, cross a track, go through a gate ahead and keep beside the hedge heading for Lodge Farm.

6.   After passing to the left of the farm, go through a gate and cross a long grass field, with the hedge on your left, to reach Plungar beside a signpost to "Stathern

Lodge". Go along Harby Lane, turn into Frog Lane and follow it to the end, then turn left along the twitchell intriguingly called "The Gas". This lovely village path brings you out beside the Belvoir Inn, which offers refreshments.

7.   Turn left to leave Plungar and join the canal, where you should follow the towpath to the right, but only as far as the next bridge, number 50. Follow Gypsy Lane to the left for nearly 2 km, and after it turns sharply left, watch out for a gate on the right, with a signpost opposite. Go through the gate, go left to cross a footbridge and enter the next field, then follow the headland to a road, coming out a stone's throw from Granby Church.

POINTS OF INTEREST

Granby:

A Roman altar was dug up in the churchyard of the church of All Saints in 1812. Granby was remarkable for giving the title of "Marquis" to the Duke of Rutland, whose ancestor purchased the estate.

The Marquis of Granby public house was named after John, the eldest son of the third Duke of Rutland who held this title. He was a popular war hero as Commander in Chief of the British Forces in Germany, and died in 1770.

The *Grantham Canal* was completed in 1797 to bring coal more cheaply from the coalfield to Grantham. Farm produce was also shipped to town, and industrial products from Grantham to its markets. The Canal was officially abandoned in 1936 due to competition from railways and road.

Lodge Farm where walkers might fancy a visit to the farmyard and the mile-long Nature Trail, or perhaps just the tearoom. This new venture re-opens in March each year.

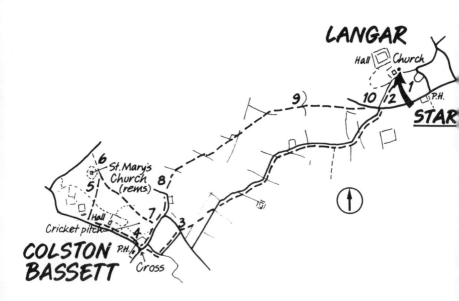

WALK 52

52. Samuel Butler Walk

A circular walk in south Nottinghamshire taking in the countryside loved by Samuel Butler, author of the book 'The Way of All Flesh'. The walk links the villages of Langar and Colston Bassett.

THE FACTS

Area:	Langar, Colston Bassett
Distance:	8 km (5 miles)
Duration:	2.5 hours
Maps Required:	OS Pathfinder 834 (SK 63/73) Radcliffe on Trent & Keyworth
	OS Landranger 129 Nottingham & Loughborough
Bus/Train Link:	Bingham
Terrain:	Across open countryside, easy walking
Starting Point:	Langar Church and village green SK 722346
Refreshments:	Martin's Arms public house and Post Office, Colston Bassett
Please note:	In paragraph 2 we describe the definitive line of the footpath. However, because the route is difficult to walk, we also describe a permissive route as an alternative. We shall be endeavouring to ensure the definitive line is properly reinstated.

THE ROUTE

1.   From facing the church, turn left, keeping the churchyard wall on your right. At the end of the churchyard, veer right onto a short track to a stile. Cross this and walk diagonally left across a field, to a gate in the far corner.

2.   Cross the road slightly right to the narrow gated road opposite. Veer right

with the road, ignoring the farm track to the left, and continue for 1/5 km passing one more track on your left. On reaching the track on the left to the Lodge, continue in the same direction for 170 metres to a gate on the right. Walk through the gate and with the gate at your back, walk diagonally left across two fields to another gate.

The definitive line at present may be difficult to follow, until the matter is rectified (see note above). An alternative is to continue along Langar Lane to a T-junction (opposite the Cheese Factory). Turn right towards Colston Bassett, and then continue at paragraph 3.

3.   Go through the gate, then turn left along the road. Turn right (Baker's Lane) and then right again (Bunystone) to arrive at a further junction. Then turn left to the village cross and post office. A public house (Martin's Arms) is available to the left.

4.   From the village cross, walk up Hall Lane, over the River Smite bridge to follow a brick wall to Colston Hall. At the end of the wall take the footpath right across Colston Hall grounds, going through trees and crossing a large lawn. Go across the drive then straight on through more trees to lead to a small metal gate, then into an open field, walking on towards a cricket pavilion.

5.   Bear left before the cricket pavilion and walk to a large wooden gate which gives access to a wide track leading to the picturesque ruins of St. Mary's Church.

6.   Retrace your steps to the Pavilion, passing to its left, or at the Cricket Club's request, walk to its right, and continue ahead aiming to the left of the church in the distance and find a bridge over a stream at the field's end.

7.   Cross over the bridge to rejoin the village street. Turn left and walk up to a road junction (Church Gate). Continue along Church Gate and just beyond the last houses of the village and continue in the same direction over the stile.

8.   Pass through the gate, then walk across the field, parallel to the fence on the left. In the next field, veer right to a gap in the hedge near the corner of the field. Continue in the same direction, under power lines to reach a stile in the field corner. Over this and pass through a gate on your right. Pass just right of a corner of trees in a small enclosure and continue to another stile. Over this, turn sharp right, to pass just left of a square enclosure containing a derelict barn, and continue bearing slightly left to a bridge.

9.   Cross the bridge over the stream, and straight ahead to a second bridge, then

walk in the same direction towards the road seen ahead, going over a third bridge and stile to access onto the road.

10. Turn right for some 30 metres to the footpath on the left. Follow the right-hand edge of the field and at the first corner turn right over a stile to follow a large metal fence on your left. Pass through the kissing gates ahead to a stile to return to the start of the walk.

POINTS OF INTEREST

Langar:

The church of St. Andrew is in Early English style, with monuments to the Chaworth family, who once owned Wiverton Hall. In the chancel are memorials to the Scroope family, including "Black Dick of Langar", the nickname of Admiral Lord Howe, a descendant of the Scroopes, who led the English navy to defeat the French in the "Battle of the Glorious First of June", a victory still celebrated in the village.

Colston Bassett:

This village stands on the border of Nottinghamshire and Leicestershire on the river Smite. From the time of Henry I the Lords of the Manor were the Bassett family, until the family name died out with Lord Ralph.

In the Civil War, several skirmish battles took place around the village. In 1625 Manor Farm housed two brothers, one loyal to the King, the other, Francis Hacker, was involved in the arrest of Charles I and escorted him to the scaffold in 1649.

The village cross dates from Medieval times, and was restored in 1831.

The church of St. John the Divine was built in Victorian Gothic style in the new estate village as a replacement for the decaying church of St. Mary, which has now disappeared.

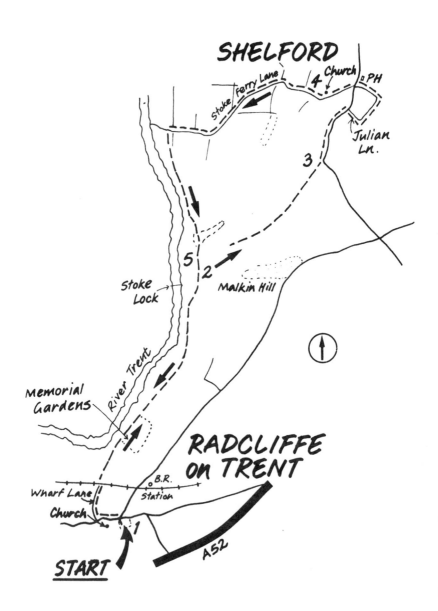

WALK 53

53. The Red Cliffs of Radcliffe

A rewarding walk over the red sandstone cliffs at Radcliffe to the isolated village of Shelford with its interesting church which originates from the 14th century.

THE FACTS

Area:	Radcliffe on Trent, Shelford
Distance:	13 km (8 miles)
Duration:	4 hours
Maps Required:	OS Pathfinder 813 (SK 64/74) Carlton & Elston and
	834 (SK 63/73) Radcliffe & Keyworth
	OS Landranger 129 Nottingham & Loughborough
Bus/Train Link:	Nottingham
Terrain:	Field paths and country lanes
Starting Point:	Main Street Car Park, Radcliffe on Trent SK646392
Refreshments:	Numerous pubs in Radcliffe; Chesterfield Arms, Shelford

THE ROUTE

1.   From the car park turn left into Main Street, then right into Wharf Lane. Pass under the railway bridge and ascend the steps, right, to join the tarmac path overlooking the Trent valley with Nottingham in the distance and Stoke Lock below. *At this point you may divert to visit the parish church and the attractive memorial gardens.*

2.   After 1.5 km, descend to an arable field, bear right along the field edge path with the hedge on your right, then left and in 150 metres right, along a farm track to meet a minor road which leads to Shelford village.

3.   Continue ahead, then turn right into Julian Lane. After 200 metres take the stile left, and proceed for 300 metres to join a farm track. Turn left to the village green. The Chesterfield Arms offers refreshments 150 metres right. Cross the road to pass the Church with its many relics to the Stanhope family who acquired the title "Earls of Chesterfield".

4.   At the crossroads turn right into Stoke Ferry Lane. After 1.5 km take the stile left, signed *The Trent Valley Way*. Follow the floodbank to rejoin your outward route at point (2), below Gibbet Hill.

5.   Retrace your steps along the cliff top walk to the car park.

POINTS OF INTEREST

Radcliffe:

The memorial gardens at Radcliffe are superb in early summer with an abundance of rhododendrons.

The church of St. Mary was built in the late 19th century. In the churchyard are good slate headstones by James Sparrow, one of the Nottinghamshire slate workers who lived and worked here.

Shelford:

The church is dedicated to St. Peter and St. Paul and is well worth a visit, especially the Stanhope Chapel, with its alabaster monuments including that of Lady Anne Stanhope who died in 1587, which is a tomb chest with her 8 children kneeling round her. The Stanhope family once occupied Shelford Manor, but nowadays most of the surrounding countryside belongs to the Crown. The manor house was built c17th-18th century, and incorporated masonry from Shelford Priory, an Augustinian Priory founded c1160.

54. Water, Water Everywhere ...!

An easy walk largely on good tracks and towpaths, including a section of the Grantham Canal. This walk could be combined with a visit to the National Water Sports Centre.

THE FACTS

Area:	Radcliffe on Trent, Basingfield, Holme Pierrepont
Distance:	9.6 km (6 miles)
Duration:	3 hours
Maps Required:	OS Pathfinder 834 (SK 63/73) Radcliffe on Trent & Keyworth
	OS Landranger 129 Nottingham & Loughborough
Bus/Train Link:	Nottingham
Terrain:	Easy, parts may be difficult after heavy rain
Starting Point:	Health Centre Car Park, Main Road, Radcliffe on Trent SK 646392
Refreshments:	Numerous pubs in Radcliffe on Trent; Shepherd's pub/cafe Stragglethorpe

THE ROUTE

1. From the car park return to the Main Road and turn left. Pass the Church, then take the next turning left onto Water Lane. Passing the end of Shadwell Grove, the road swings right. Shortly beyond, turn left onto a narrow path between houses. At the end of this, turn right, then left at a T-junction. At the next junction continue ahead into St. Lawrence Boulevard, and shortly after passing two more streets on your left, turn left at a footpath sign to follow another narrow path between fences, to emerge on the A52 trunk road.

2. **Cross with care** to a footpath sign opposite. Go through the gap in the hedge,

turn left and then shortly right to follow a dyke. At the end of the dyke the path begins to veer right towards a hedge, reaching it just before the brow of the hill. Cross into the adjoining field and turn left along the hedge. As the path starts to descend veer right again to a bridge over Polser Brook. Cross this and continue ahead across the narrow end of a large field. Turn right before the hedge and continue with the hedge on your left for three fields to reach a road alongside the Cocked Hat Plantation.

3.   Turn left along the road for 300 metres then turn right at a bridleway sign (opposite the sign for North Farm). Follow a broad grassy track along a field edge, cross a railway line and continue to reach a road. Turn left for 600 metres to reach the Grantham Canal.

4.   Cross the bridge and turn right along the towpath for almost 2 km. When the houses of Basingfield come into view, look for a concrete footbridge over the Canal. Cross this, and continue on an obvious track into the village. Turn right at the road then immediately follow it round to the left. Shortly before this road reaches the A52, turn right at a footpath sign to follow to the right of a hedge. Cross a stile on your left and cross a field to another stile half-way along the right-hand fence. Turn left to the A52, then right along it for a few metres and cross to a metalled lane just beyond a bus shelter.

5.   Follow the lane past a large double gate (there's a stile to the left) and where it swings left, veer right at a footpath sign to follow a way-marked path beside a man-made lake. Continue ahead in the next field at the end of which turn left over a stile to continue beside the lake. Later the track becomes a narrow bank with water on both sides, then crosses a brook to emerge in a minor road.

6.   Turn right to follow Adbolton Lane for 1.4 km back to Radcliffe, keeping straight ahead at all junctions, passing Holme Pierrepont Hall and church. On reaching a T-junction opposite a bus depot, turn left back to the centre of the village.

POINTS OF INTEREST

Holme Pierrepont National Watersport Centre: created from a series of gravel pits on the south bank of the river Trent, this was opened in the early 1970's, and offers support facilities for all watersport enthusiasts.

Holme Pierrepoint Hall: family seat of the Dukes of Kingston and Earl Manvers.

The small church of St. Edmund nearby contains numerous family monuments.

Radcliffe on Trent:

The Memorial Gardens are superb in early summer with an abundance of rhododendrons.

The church of St. Mary was built in the late 19th century. In the churchyard are good slate headstones by James Sparrow, one of the Nottinghamshire slate workers who lived and worked here.

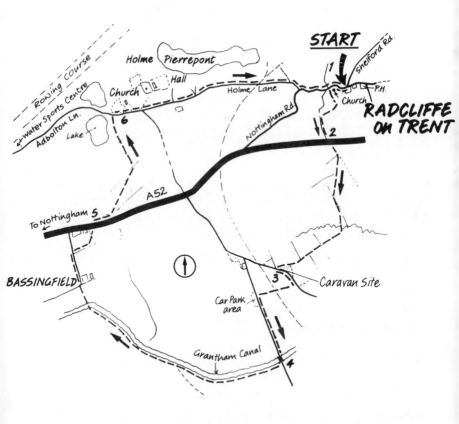

WALK 54

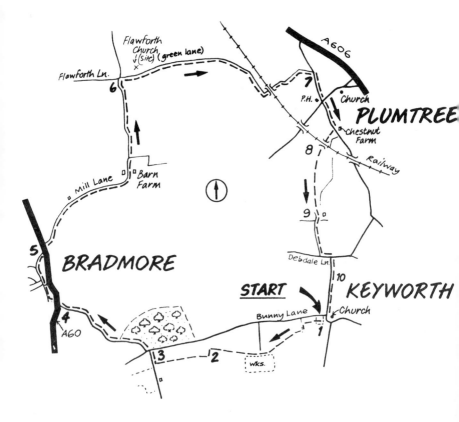

Flawforth
Church
√ (site) (**green lane**)
×

Flawforth Ln.

6

7

P.H. •

A606

Church

PLUMTREE

8

Chestnut
Farm

Railway

Mill Lane

Barn
Farm

9

BRADMORE

Debdale Ln.

5

START

10

KEYWORTH

Church

4

A60

Bunny Lane

1

3

2

wks.

WALK 55

55. Wandering in the South Nottinghamshire Wolds

A bracing walk over the South Nottinghamshire Wolds taking in the site of the ancient remains of Flawforth Church and the picturesque villages of Bradmore and Plumtree.

THE FACTS

Area:	Flawforth, Bradmore, Plumtree
Distance:	12 km (7.5 miles)
Duration:	3.75 hours
Maps Required:	OS Pathfinder 833 (SK 43/53) Nottingham South West and OS 834 (SK 63/73) Ratcliffe on Trent & Keyworth
	OS Landranger 129 Nottingham & Loughborough
Bus/Train Link:	Nottingham
Terrain:	Farm road, green lane and field path. Easy walking with distant views.
Starting Point:	Shoppers' Car Park off Bunny Lane, Keyworth SK 613308
Refreshments:	Public Houses in Plumtree and Keyworth

THE ROUTE

1. From the car park, walk to the opposite end to the car entry and exit point, and turn right onto a tarmac path. After 50 metres take the path forking left into Wright's Orchard cul-de-sac. After a further 50 metres, there is a twitchell on the right-hand side, leading to Brookview Drive. Walk diagonally left across the Drive, past a small, triangular green to continue along the twitchell which leads to a stile.

2.   Cross the stile and follow the field path with the hedge on your right. After the second field, cross over another stile and continue to the sewage works which will be on your left. You will then reach a wooden footbridge, where you turn right through a metal field gate, then left with a wire fence on your left. At the end of this pasture, step over the wire fence on the left and after 10 metres go over a wooden footbridge on the right.

3.   Step over another wire fence into another pasture and continue in the same direction facing Ratcliffe Power Station in the distance. At the end of this field, go through a metal farm gate onto the Wysall Road, where you turn right. Continue to the road junction and go ahead along Pendock Lane to Bradmore for about 1.2 km.

4.   At the T-junction with the A60, go straight across to a concrete drive and then over a stile with a concrete wall on your right. Cross over another stile, and turn right to walk between farm buildings and a house garden, then over a stile leading to Farmer Street, which you follow for 500 metres to rejoin the main A60 road.

5.   Turn left onto the A60 and in 100 metres on the right-hand side is Mill Lane, a bridleway. Follow this for 2 km, passing Barn Farm and continuing ahead to reach Flawforth Lane.

6.   At this point, Flawforth Lane turns sharp left. Ignore this, and walk across a lay-by on the right to the ancient site of Flawforth Church of St. Peter. After visiting the church, go across the site to the far right-hand corner and exit onto a bridleway with the hedge on your right. After four fields, the bridleway becomes enclosed with hedges on both sides. Turn left under an old railway line and continue to the road at Plumtree Cottage.

7.   Here you turn right and proceed through Plumtree village, past the crossroads with the Griffin Inn on your right, where you have the chance of a well-deserved rest, and Plumtree School on your left. After about 250 metres there is a stile on the right, opposite Chestnut Farm. The path goes through a railway arch.

8.   On the other side of the arch go straight ahead across a field and make for the corner of a hedge. Continue along with the hedge on your left, shortly crossing a wooden footbridge, then with the hedge on your right for 20 metres, go through a hedge opening and turn left with the hedge on your left and walk up the hill. At the top of the field turn around to look at the fine view of the Wolds.

9.   At the top of the field there is a narrow path going right and then left around

the perimeter of a school and garden boundaries, leading into Crossdale Drive. Turn right (the school entrance being on the left) and walk along Crossdale Drive. Between nos. 5 and 7 a twitchell leads to Nottingham Road, beside the Fairway public house.

10. Turn right and then left along Nottingham Road towards Keyworth church, with Bunny Lane on the right and the car park immediately on the left.

POINTS OF INTEREST

Keyworth:

The church of St. Mary Magdalene has an unusual tower which in the 15th century was used as a beacon to guide travellers across the wolds.

Bradmore:

The village is linked with Bunny, as the Parkyns family of Bunny purchased it from the Willoughbys of Wollaton. There was a serious fire in 1706 which destroyed much of the village, including the church which was never rebuilt, as the village came under the jurisdiction of the vicar of Bunny. Sir Thomas Parkyns, the wrestling baron rebuilt the village after the great fire.

Flawforth Church:

The original parish church fell into disuse in the 18th century as the population migrated.

Plumtree:

A commuter village typical of the Wolds countryside. The parish church of St. Mary is believed to lie on the site of a 9th century church. The present building has sections of Saxon brickwork, with Norman doorways on the west tower. Stones to repair the tower came from the old Trent Bridge.

Much of the building work and improvements in the village were undertaken by the Burnside family, and the initials of W.E. Burnside may be seen on several buildings. The family built the school, the Griffin Inn, the post office, a farm and finally the Burnside Memorial Hall.

56. Bunny Hop!

A circular walk taking in Bunny Woods, excellent views of Charnwood Fore and South Nottinghamshire and around East Leake and along the Fairham Brool

THE FACTS

Area:	Bunny, East Leake
Distance:	13 km (8 miles)
Duration:	4 hours
Maps Required:	OS Pathfinder (SK 42/52) Loughborough North
	OS Landranger 129 Nottingham & Loughborough
Bus/Train Link:	Nottingham
Terrain:	Some of the paths used can be very muddy in winter.
Starting Point:	Park with care in Church Street, Bunny SK 582296
Refreshments:	Rancliffe Arms, Bunny and shops in East Leake

THE ROUTE

1.   From Church Street walk along Loughborough Road (A60) through Bunn past the Rancliffe Arms, over Fairham Brook Bridge and out of the village to reac a group of houses on the right. Cross the road and take the lane on the left. After 5 metres turn right, and past a steel barrier gate. Walk up the concrete road toward the closed Silver Seal Gypsum Mine. On reaching the disused working area, tak the path on the left past two buildings. Continue ahead to rejoin the concrete roac then take the hedged path going uphill on the left. At the top of the rise turn righ then left over ditchboards to walk and enter Bunny Old Wood Nature Reserv Turn right and walk along the bridleway to walk out of the wood and rejoin th A60 at Bunny Hill.

2.   Turn left for 40 metres and cross the road **with care**. Go up the road opposit

(Bunny Hill Top) going past houses and the School of National Equitation to rejoin the roadside pavement. Continue ahead past the bus shelter to reach Ash Lane.

3.   Walk along Ash Lane passing several houses. Ignore all turns to the left and right: we eventually come into an open field, with distant views of Charnwood Forest seen to the half-left. Continue ahead to the next field, just before Hill Top Farm. Turn left and follow the field edge path around to the right-hand corner of the field. Excellent views here. Over the stile, then go diagonally right aiming in the direction of East Leake Fire Station Tower seen ahead, crossing two fields to reach a stile in the field corner. Over the stile and track and cross the field diagonally, to take the stile to the right of Taft Leys Farm.

4.   Go straight over the track to enter the field opposite (take care with the ditch). Go across the field diagonally left aiming for the right corner and field gate. Continue in the next field aiming for the stile to the left of the gate seen ahead left of the disused building.

5.   Turn right and walk along Lantern Lane past the school to reach Gotham Road. Cross the road and take the footpath at the side of the bus shelter. Cross the corner of the first field to a stile, then straight across the next field aiming for a second gap in the hedge on the right. Turn left, going over a bridge over Kingston Brook. Continue ahead to a stile and field gate. Continue straight ahead along a hardcore track to arrive at Main Street, East Leake (turn right to visit the Church of St. Mary). There are several public houses on Main Street.

6.   Our route turns left to walk along Main Street, past Gotham Lane continuing ahead along Costock Road. Take the footpath opposite Meeting House Close.

7.   Cross the field diagonally to the right to the corner of the conifer hedge. Walk right alongside the hedge to reach a stile. Over the stile, then go diagonally left and walk to the right-hand corner of the field, over the stile onto Sheep Lank Lane, going over the bridge once again crossing Kingston Brook. Take the parallel right-hand green track and where both tracks merge, look for a gap in the hedge some 40 metres on the right.

8.   Climb the fence to enter the field going diagonally left aiming for a gap in the hedge in the middle of the field. Go left across the next field to reach a gate and farm track.

9.   Turn right along Lantern Lane then left after 70 metres. Walk past Taft Leys

Farm (previously visited) and continue along a broad green lane climbing uphill (Hotchley Hill). At the top of the hill the green lane drops downhill to reach a footpath on the right as the lane bends left.

10. Cross the ditchboard, then go diagonally left across the field to the field entrance in the field corner, aiming to the left of the wooded hills, then cross Gotham Lane to enter the field opposite. Go diagonally right aiming for a gap in the hedge to the right-hand corner. Go over a culvert bridge into the next field, then half-diagonally left aiming for a marker post to reach a bridleway. Turn sharp right and walk along the bridleway to reach the bridleway bridge. We continue straight on at this piont across the field (ignore the path to the right and soon after to the left). Our route eventually reaches the banks of Fairham Brook.

11. Turn right and follow the footpath along the bank of Fairham Brook. On arriving at the bridge over Fairham Brook, cross this then go diagonally right across the field aiming for houses seen ahead to enter Main Street, Bunny.

12. Walk down Main Street. At the junction just before Bunny Post Office, you can turn left along Church Street to return to your car or go straight on to the Rancliffe Arms public house.

POINTS OF INTEREST

Bunny:

The name derives from an old English term for the reeds or long grasses that grew in this area. The village's most famous son was Thomas Parkyns, an 18th century eccentric scholar, lawyer, amateur architect and benefactor. The family had been connected with the village since 1570. Thomas designed and built many of the farmhouses in the district; the wall around Bunny Hall, which was built on a series of arches; the old school house and almshouses. He was known as the "Wrestling Baronet", as in 1712 he established an annual wrestling match on Midsummer's Day, a tradition which continued for 99 years. He often competed himself. He designed his own monument, which stands in the parish church, depicting himself life-size in a wrestling stance.St. Mary's Church is often regarded as "The Cathedral of the Wolds" and dates from the 14th century, although Sir Thomas restored and reroofed much of it.

East Leake:

The Post Office was originally the old Manor House, built between 1715 and 1728.

192

The church of St. Mary was mentioned in the Domesday Book and stands on the site of much older buildings, being extensively restored in the nineteenth century. In the church is the 8 feet Vamp Horn, known in the village as "The Shawm". Only five other churches have such an instrument, which was invented in 1670 by Samuel Morland, one of Samuel Pepys' tutors at Cambridge and was used by the bass singer to lead the choir from the gallery to the church. Two Roundheads and three Cavaliers were killed in a skirmish locally in 1644, and they lie in unmarked graves near the church porch.

The small village green has a brook running past the war memorial, and there are the remains of the village pound, now furnished with seats. For a number of years there has been an annual tug-of-war across the brook which has developed into a carnival parade.

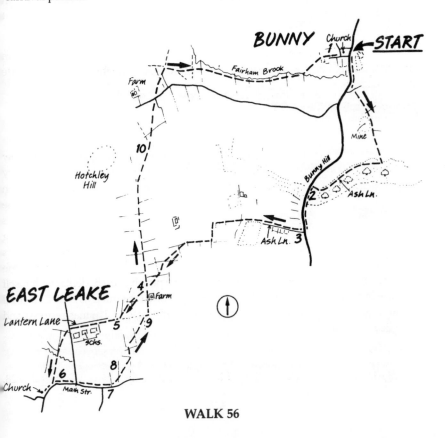

WALK 56

57. Barton (In The Beans) and the Gotham Ridge

This short walk joins two delightful villages in the Trent valley before climbing to the ridge of Gotham Hill. There are wide-ranging views from the ridge towards Gotham to the east and Nottingham to the west.

THE FACTS

Area:	Barton in Fabis, Thrumpton
Distance:	7.5 km (4.5 miles)
Duration:	2.25 hours
Maps Required:	OS Pathfinder 833 (SK 43/53) Nottingham (South West)
	OS Landranger 129 Nottingham & Loughborough
Bus/Train Link:	Nottingham
Terrain:	One steep climb. Can get muddy after rain.
Starting Point:	Barton-in-Fabis Church SK 523327
Refreshments:	None on the route

THE ROUTE

1.   Starting with your back to Barton Church, turn right, then after a hundred metres right again at Rectory Place. After 50 metres cross the stile left, cross the old farmyard to another stile and follow the grass path across the field. Cross the floodbank and continue to the gate in the corner.

2.   Pass through the slip-stile and turn left to follow the field edge around a loop to another gate. Pass through the hand-gate and follow the edge of two grass fields to the riverside. Follow the farm-track by the Trent: the track becomes a tarmac road which passes the gatehouse to Thrumpton Hall. *Before leaving the village take the opportunity to visit All Saints' Church and return to the gate on the right.* Soon after

this gatehouse go through a gate left, forward to a stile and across three fields, aiming for a lone house.

3.   On reaching the road, turn right for 100 metres and left over a bridge. *You can now shorten the walk slightly by turning left, then right up the hill along a grassy path and diagonally through Gotham Hill Wood.*

4.   Our route goes right on a bridleway, up the hill past Hillside Cottage and immediately right to a field gate. After a gate, swing left up the hill and pass through Cottagers Hill Spinney. At the top, take a well-deserved rest, enjoying the view from the advantage of the seat. Then, turn left along the edge of the wood, with views across to Gotham and the Soar Valley. Pass through a gate at the end of the wood to join the shorter route and continue along the field edge.

5.   Go through a gate, then cross a stile to the left, at the corner of Long Spinney. You are now on a diverted route, skirting to the left of a pig farm following the clear way-marks, rejoining a track at the other side leading past Glebe Farm to the road. * Continue along the road ahead to return to Barton Church and cross the first field to a stile for panoramic views of the Trent Valley and also Nottingham ahead.

   * *We are aware that due to the upgrading of the A453, this path will be diverted.*

POINTS OF INTEREST

Barton-in-Fabis:

The village was also known as Barton-in-the-Beans and was described by Sir Osbert Sitwell, in his book "Tales my Father taught me" as one of the three Sacheverell villages, with Ratcliffe-on-Soar and Morley (Derbyshire) being the other two.

The church of St. George dates from the late 14th century and contains monuments to the Sacheverell family.

There is a brick, octagonal dovecote in the farmyard of the former Manor house (now a plant nursery), which was built by the Sacheverells in the late 17th century.

At Glebe Farm, the remains of a Roman Villa were excavated in 1856 and 1949. Two mosaic floors were revealed.

At Brands Hill there are the remains of Medieval contour ploughing with lynchets or small banks used to makr the boundaries of the small plots.

Thrumpton:

Thrumpton Hall was built in the 17th century and is situated with beautiful grounds alongside the River Trent. The Hall has connections with Byron family and some of their graves can be found in the nearby churchyard.

All Saints Church was of Medieval origin, but has been much restored and rebuilt in the 19th century. There is a decaying Medieval font in the churchyard.

In the village, almost all the gabled brick houses were built c1700-45 by John Emerton of the Hall, whose initials are carved on the datestones. These are fine examples of early 18th century estate building.

Gotham Hill, a site of special scientific interest, overlooks the Trent valley.

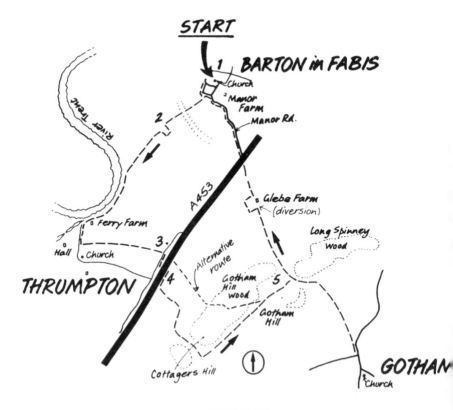

WALK 57

58. Kingston Brook Circular

A circular walk taking in Wysall, the Medieval village site of Thorpe in the Glebe and Willoughby on the Wolds.

THE FACTS

Area:	Wysall, Thorpe in the Glebe, Willoughby on the Wolds
Distance:	10 km (6.5 miles) including visit to Willoughby
	8.5 km (5.5 miles) if Willoughby is not visited
Duration:	3.5 hours or 3 hours if shorter option is taken
Maps Required:	OS Pathfinder 853 (SK 42/52) Loughborough North & Castle Donington and 854 (SK 62/72) Scalford & Nether Broughton
	OS Landranger 129 Nottingham & Loughborough
Bus/Train Link:	Loughborough
Terrain:	Fairly level, mixture of pasture and arable, with wooded areas
Starting Point:	Wysall Church (park carefully in the village) SK 604271
Refreshments:	Public houses in Wysall and Willoughby
Special Notes:	**This walk takes you on a public Right of Way: however, YOU MUST NOT LEAVE THE OFFICIAL PATH, must not make any explorations or use metal detectors, nor use the site for picnics - the landowner will not permit any site visits. Please respect his wishes.**
	In paragraph 3, at the time of writing, the path from the gate past the pylon to the corner of the field is likely to be cropped out. We shall endeavour to have the path properly reinstated.

197

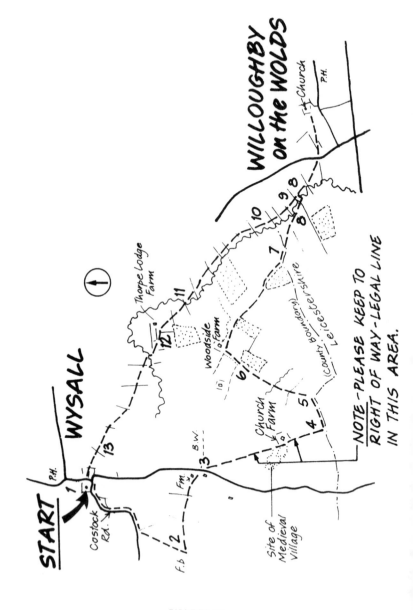

WALK 58

THE ROUTE

1.   Facing the church, walk left along Costock Road for 0.5 km going as far as Elm Lodge. Take the footpath opposite on the left. Enter a field, and aim across to the telegraph pole seen ahead to the right of the pylon. After reaching the pole, walk to the footbridge now visible ahead and slightly to the right. *(Please note: we are walking the legal line).*

2.   We now return back across the field in an easterly direction aiming just left of the previous pylon, then continue in the same direction to a hedge over a stile, with the hedge on the right, towards Windyridge Farm. As the hedge goes left, go over a stile to take the track to the right of the farm house.

3.   On reaching the road go through the gate opposite. Our path goes diagonally right across the field, aiming to the right of a pylon and to the right-hand corner of the field (see note above). Go over two stiles and a stream and cross the field aiming for Church Site Farm seen ahead. *We must again emphasize: PLEASE KEEP TO THE RIGHT OF WAY. Do not leave the legal line. We must stress the landowner does not allow any site visits or explorations and asks you to leave the site as quickly as possible.* On reaching the stile go over this and aim directly towards the farm gate adjoining the outbuilding to the left of the farm house.

4.   Go through the gate and turn left, then ahead diagonally directly across the field to a stile. In the next field aim for a further stile in its right-hand corner.

5.   Over the stile, turn left and follow the field edge to a stile. *You are now in Leicestershire for a short period.* Go over the stile and through the adjacent gate. In the next field turn left with the gate at your back and walk diagonally right to reach a stile. Over this, and straight across the field to a gate and ditchboard over a stream. Straight on following the field edge path (hedge on right), past a plantation, until you reach the farm gate.

6.   Go straight on towards Woodside Farm. Just before reaching the farm a path joins from the left. We turn right at this point and walk in a straight direction, aiming to just left of Jubilee Plantation to reach the farm gate. Through this to continue straight on. At the end of the Plantation, bear right to pass through another farm gate.

7.   Turn left and follow the field edge path (hedge on left) until you reach two stiles and ditchboards, just before a gate. Over these, then turn right following the

field edge path to the left of Triangle Plantation, to reach a further farm gate. Continue straight on, past two further farm gates *(you are now re-entering Leicestershire).*

8.   Bear left to reach a farm gate. Head diagonally to a gate just visible in the right-hand hedge. Go through this and head left across the field to its far left corner. Through a farm gate and then adjacent to a pylon, cross over Kingston Brook by a pylon. *Please note: to return quickly to Wysall a left turn is taken here (see Section 9). We however recommend a visit into Willoughby on the Wolds and in particular to visit St. Mary's and All Saints' Church.*

8a.   If following the extension into Willoughby on the Wolds, go right to follow the brook to a stile, which you cross, then walk diagonally across the field to the far right corner. Over the stile, onto the road and take the footpath on the left. Go over the stile, then follow the field edge path on the right to a further stile. Over this walk right, past a pond, to a stile, which you go over and then aim downhill to cross the stream and enter the churchyard. After your visit to the Church and Willoughby on the Wolds, return to point 8 at Kingston Brook.

9.   Turn left (right if returning from Willoughby) to follow the brook (hedge on left) going over two stiles with ditchboards between. Go straight across the next field to two further stiles *(note you are on the route of the Midshires Way: a long distance walk from the Ridgeway to the Trans-Pennine Trail).* Head straight over the next field to a further stile to go straight on to reach a track. Go over this to reach two more stiles and ditchboards. Straight across the next field to a further stile.

10.   We now follow the brook, to reach the field corner. Go over the stile on the left and walk down to the brook and to reach a stile and ditchboard on the right. Keep to the left through the next field crossing a stile onto the road. Cross the road over the stile and keep left parallel with the brook. Bear slightly left as the brook soon curves away. Cross the next fence and walk to the footbridge on the left.

11.   Turn right over the bridge then turn right to a stile. Over this, then bear diagonally left to the far left field corner to the left of Thorpe Lodge Farm.

12.   Go over the stile, and follow the hedge on the right to reach a stile on the right corner of the field. Go over the footbridge then bear diagonally left to reach stiles and ditchboards. Go straight on in the next field to further stiles and ditchboards. In the next field bear diagonally right to reach a stile three-quarters of the way along the hedge at the end of the field, from the left-hand corner.

13. Over this stile, then over the steps in the fence on your right. You are now entering a horse paddock area. Go left towards the church, and over the stile at the end of the field. Straight on and go over two stiles with footbridges in between. Follow the field on the left-hand side to a stile in the corner. Over the stile to a gap between buildings to come onto the street by the church.

POINTS OF INTEREST

Wysall:

This small village has survived since before the Domesday Book, with around 300 inhabitants. A fine clock on the church tower was erected after the First World War to celebrate the safe return of all the village men.

Thorpe in the Glebe:

This is one of the best deserted Medieval village sites in the Midlands, although the earthworks of a long sunken road with rectangular enclosures on each side are preserved under grass. The remains of the church, which was still in use in 1743, lie in the farmyard of Churchside Farm.

Willoughby on the Wolds:

The village stands near the Leicestershire border, the name originating from the Danish word *Wilgebi* which means village of the willows. Nearby is a site of a Roman settlement *Vernemetum*, and an Anglo-Saxon burial ground.

During the Civil War a minor battle was fought in a field near the church, where a Royalist officer was buried. Legend says that the villagers climbed the church tower to watch the battle, and the brook ran red with blood!

Church of St. Mary and All Saints is about 800 years old, with a 14th century chantry chapel containing some amazing alabaster tombs, together with other items of interest.

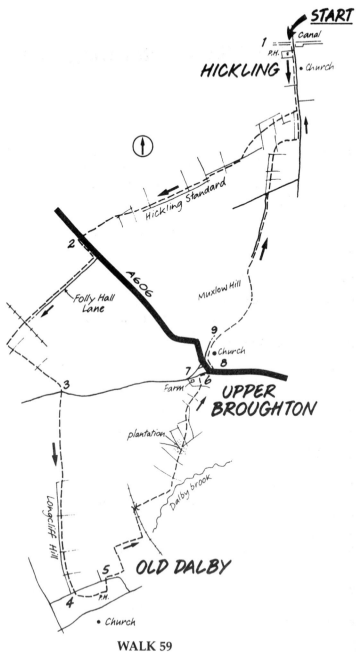

WALK 59

59. The Belvoir Ridgeway

An airy walk along the ridges of Hickling Standard and Longcliffe Hill giving magnificent views of South Nottinghamshire and neighbouring Leicestershire, together with a visit to the picturesque village of Old Dalby.

THE FACTS

Area: Hickling, Old Dalby, Upper Broughton

Distance: 15 km (9.5 miles)

Duration: 4.75 hours

Maps Required: OS Pathfinder 854 (SK 62/72) Scalford & Nether Broughton
                  OS Landranger 129 Nottingham & Loughborough

Bus/Train Link: Bingham

Terrain: Field paths and bridleways which can be muddy after rain. Undulating wolds countryside.

Starting Point: Canal Basin, Hickling SK 690295

Refreshments: Pubs in Hickling, Old Dalby and Upper Broughton

THE ROUTE

1.   From the canal basin walk through the village and 70 metres past the road to Long Clawson turn right at a footpath sign to go between houses then across a field bearing half-left. Ascend the defined path up onto Hickling Standard, admiring the view in every direction. At the top, over the stile and along the ridge, first with a hedge right then left, for just over 1 km to meet the A606.

2.   Turn left along the main road for 250 metres then right along Folly Hall Lane. 200 metres past Folly Hall cross over the railway and when the track bears right continue forward for 200 metres to hedge, when you turn left and after 1 km emerge onto a road.

203

3.   Cross over the road veering left to a bridleway sign to follow a clear track along the field edge for 600 metres, then turn left and immediately right to continue in the same direction for 1.5 km to a road.

4.   Cross over to a gated field track which bears left into Old Dalby and a pub, where you turn left to past the end of Hawthorn Close and come to a T-junction. Turn right and in 250 metres just past a right-hand bend take the footpath left.

5.   Follow the way-marks around two sides of the field then right over a stream and in 300 metres turn left along the bottom of a railway embankment. In 100 metres cross another stream then after a further 200 metres turn right through a tunnel under the railway. On the far side bear right and over a stile into the corner of a field. Turn left, to initially follow a hedge left for 150 metres, to a bridge left and over this to follow the right hand side of three fields and Dalby Brook.

6.   At a new plantation turn left to a stile and cross two more fields diagonally aiming for the far left hand corner of the second field. Cross the stile to follow a hedge right to a footbridge, then forward ascending to another stile right. Over this bear left to a further stile in the opposite hedge and continuing in the same direction pass to the right of a farm, crossing another stile to the road at Upper Broughton.

7.   Cross the road, turn right and take the twitchell on the left after Bottom Green Cottage up Well Lane to arrive at Top Green. Turn right and walk to the A606. Cross the road **with care** to take the road to the left of the Golden Fleece public house, past the village water pump. Turn left at the twitchell and walk down the side of St. Luke's church, which is worth a visit. At the next junction, turn right walking past several houses to arrive at a metal field gate on the left at the entrance to a gravel drive.

8.   Go through the gate, follow the right-hand fence to reach a further stile. Go over this and walk down the field with the hedge on your right to join a path coming in from the right across the next field. On joining this path, do not go over the stile, but turn left to cross the field to a double stile and ditchboard. Cross the next field aiming for the right-hand corner of the field and farm buildings.

9.   *At the time of writing, the next path is subject to a diversion order. We describe the route proposed, but look carefully for waymarks.* Go through the gate into the farmyard, following the track to the right of the farm buildings to reach a stile. Over this, take the stile opposite into a tree enclosure. Walk straight on to take the stile on the left.

By this time you have passed the farm buildings. Walk across the rear farmyard aiming for a further tree enclosure on the farmyard/field boundary to the right. Walk past two gates to reach a stile. Over this and walk into the tree enclosure, go over the stile and then across a further field to the half-left to reach a stile/gate and road.

10. Follow the road with care for 1.5 km to a T-junction. Turn right and immediately left at a footpath sign. Follow the hedge left through three fields then forward for 50 metres to a stile on the right. Cross this, then continue to a gate in the far left-hand corner of the field to join a track and the road. Turn left through Hickling for 1 km back to the Canal Basin.

POINTS OF INTEREST

The *Grantham Canal* is 33 miles long linking the River Trent at Nottingham and the River Witham at Grantham. Although construction work started in 1793 it was not until 1797 that it was open to traffic. The last commercial boat used the Canal in 1917. Nowadays the Canal is maintained by British Waterways, whilst a restoration society is very active with the aim of opening up the entire length for navigation.

Hickling Standard and **Longcliffe Hill** both offer the walker superb all-round views of the delightful wolds countryside on the Notts/Leics border, while *Upper Broughton* and **Old Dalby** are two picturesque villages typical of the area.

Upper Broughton:

The parish church of St. Luke is worth a visit. The village has several timber-framed cottages, such as the 17th century Willow Cottage. The village appeared in the Domesday Book and was once the site of a Roman settlement.

60. Co-operative Walk

A circular walk on the Nottinghamshire/Leicestershire boundary offering excellent views and linking the Hoton Ridge, Rempstone, St. Peter's Church, Stanford Hall and the King's Brook.

THE FACTS

Area:	Stanford on Soar, Cotes, Hoton, Rempstone	
Distance:	Long Walk	12 km (7.5 miles)
	Short Walk	7 km (4.5 miles)
Duration:	Long Walk	3.5 hours
	Short Walk	2.5 hours
Maps Required:	OS Pathfinder 853 (SK 42/52) Loughborough (North) and Castle Donington	
	OS Landranger 129 Nottingham & Loughborough	
Bus/Train Link:	Loughborough	
Terrain:	Field and riverside paths	
Starting Point:	Grass verge along Cotes Lane SK 548214	
Refreshments:	Long walk: White Lion public house, Rempstone; pub at Hoton	
	Short walk: pub at Hoton	

THE ROUTE

1.   If walking from the village of Stanford on Soar, take the road towards Cotes walking over King's Brook, ignoring two paths on the left but continue up the lane towards Moat Hill Spinney seen ahead. When coming in line with the spinney, take the green lane walking uphill towards the trees.

2.   Continue to climb firstly uphill towards the spinney, then to follow a field edge path along a clear ridge for 2.5 km. *You have excellent views all around, particularly of Stanford Hall, now the home of the International Co-operative Movement, and also Charnwood Forest may be seen to the south.* The bridleway eventually sweeps down right towards Hoton. At this point you are able to walk to the pub at Hoton for refreshments, but our route leaves the bridleway and goes into the field ahead.

3.   Turn left and drop downhill following a field edge path to reach the path at the side of the King's Brook (on the Nottinghamshire/Leicestershire boundary).

3a.   **If you are following the short route:** turn left and walk along the footpath at the side of King's Brook for 450 metres to reach a bridleway crossing where the long route joins. Move to paragraph 11.

4.   If on the long walk, turn right and walk on the field edge path at the side of King's Brook to reach the A60 (Loughborough to Nottingham road) at the Nottinghamshire/Leicestershire boundary sign.

5.   Turn left and cross the road **with considerable care** as our path is found between two chevrons on a bend in the road. Cross diagonally left towards the hedge and take the path uphill to the far corner. Turn right and walk 30 metres to a stile (note the view at this point).

6.   Cross the stile and follow the left-hand field boundary down into the village of Rempstone.

7.   Cross the road, with the White Lion public house on the left. Our route is to the right to take a footpath just before the Parish Hall. Climb straight uphill to the far left corner of the field to reach a kissing gate. Turn left along the lane for 30 metres to take a twitchell around a new development to link onto the footpath still bordering a new housing estate, to reach the A60. Turn left and walk to traffic lights.

8.   Cross the road and take the A6006 past All Saints Church, taking the path on the right by going into the Church car park. Go through a gap in a posted and wire fence near the field hedge and cross a large field aiming in a NNW direction and taking the first left-hand cooling tower of Ratcliffe-on-Soar power station as a guide. When three-quarters over the field you will see a field boundary hedge ahead with a stile seen 50 metres from a corner hedge.

9.   Over the stile into the sacred church remains of St. Peter's Church. Spend

some time here. Our route continues by walking to the far left-hand corner. Over a double stile, walk in a straight line across a field to reach the road with access through a gate.

Please note: the bridleway from St. Peter's Church is subject to a mineral planning application diversion order. We shall negotiate for an alternative path to be created that will be clearly way-marked.

10.   Turn right and walk 300 metres to cross the Melton road near the road junction to take the footpath along the field edge path. On reaching the track, turn left and take the bridleway walking to a field gate where you turn left through a bridlegate and then follow the brick boundary and walk across three fields. In the next field we have a choice whether to walk straight on down to the King's Brook to rejoin the short route. At the time of writing, there is no bridge crossing the King's Brook at this point. If it is in flood take this alternative route:

10a. Turn right on entering the fourth field, walk to the end of the boundary wall then turn left to reach a culvert bridge and aim for the corner of the field and a stile. Cross this to enter shrub-land. Follow the way-marked posts through this area to reach a concrete bridge over the King's Brook.

11.   If you have rejoined the short route by crossing King's Brook at the earlier crossing, turn right and walk on field edge path to join the route described in 12a at the junction near the concrete bridge.

12.   We now all follow the field edge path, following the King's Brook back to Stanford on Soar. On reaching the road you turn right to reach the village or turn left to return to the start of the walk.

POINTS OF INTEREST

Stanford on Soar:

The church of St. John the Baptist dates from the 13th century. There are several interesting monuments in the church, such as the incised slab to an Illyngworth and his wife dated 1408, which is unique because it is the only alabaster slab in the county with indents for brass inlays. There is also a recumbent effigy holding his heart in his hand.

Stanford Hall, standing in a landscaped park, was the brick mansion of Charles Vere Dashwood.

Rempstone:

The church of All Saints was consecrated in 1773 and has many of the original furnishings, including the squire's pew.

Earthworks at Sheepwash Brook show where the village originally stood. It gradually migrated half a mile to its present location.

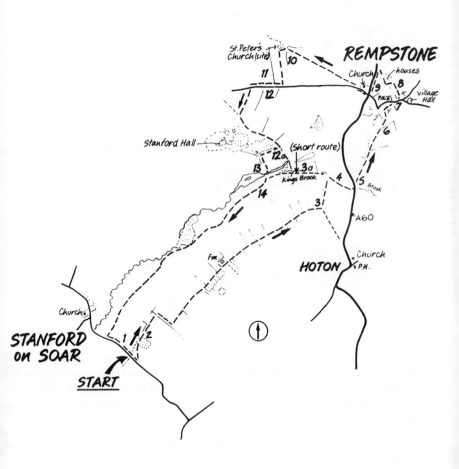

WALK 60